Mrs Musterman

MILLINER OF MAIN STREET

a biography

ELIZABETH LEAH REED

Mrs. Musterman—Milliner of Main Street: A Biography

Copyright © 2021 Elizabeth Leah Reed. All rights reserved. No part of this book may be reproduced or retransmitted in any form or by any means without the written permission of the publisher.

Published by Wheatmark®
2030 East Speedway Boulevard, Suite 106
Tucson, Arizona 85719 USA
www.wheatmark.com

Biography, Women, Business, Milliner, Immigrants, History—Maryland

ISBN: 978-1-62787-854-8 (Paperback)
ISBN: 978-1-62787-855-5 (ebook)
LCCN: 2020922267

Bulk ordering discounts are available through Wheatmark, Inc. For more information, email orders@wheatmark.com or call 1-888-934-0888.

Book design by Lori Conser
Cover photo by James Thomas Reed

So you may know her too

Reed, Michael, Lene, Alexandra, Luke,
Anna, Brian, Amy, and Isaac

To remember the past is to make it present again.

—Fernando Pessao

CONTENTS

FOREWORD

*M*ARYLAND IS OFTEN CALLED "America in Miniature" because its geography spans from the sandy
beaches of the Atlantic Ocean to the remnants
of the eroding Appalachian Mountains on its western bor-
der. Annapolis, the state's capital, may be called "America's
cultural history in miniature." Settled in 1649, the city has
stories to tell about our country's Founding Fathers as well as
about those of the ordinary people who shaped the town as
the country grew and changed.

It is the ordinary people, whose names are often unknown
or forgotten, who built and continue to build our communi-
ties. But when they pass on their stories and legacies to family and friends they enrich our lives in many unknown ways.
The book *Mrs. Musterman—Milliner of Main Street: A Biography*
describes one such "ordinary" woman, one who left a legacy
and had an extraordinary impact on family, friends, and all
who met her.

In this biography, Elizabeth Leah Reed does a masterful
job describing the life of a twentieth-century milliner—her
grandmother—and the forces that shaped her. From stories

of her Colonial Era ancestors, her early life on the nineteenth-century Eastern Shore of Virginia, and her apprenticeship, to the descriptions of the challenges she faced as a woman in business, this book reveals experiences and historic circumstances unknown to us today. With powerful writing throughout *Mrs. Musterman—Milliner*, the author unveils and honors the specialness of family history, the stories we each must discover and tell to maintain our personal legacies. It is the discovery in the research and the telling that strengthens and inspires us to goodness.

Lillian Musterman, hat shop owner from 1921 to 1967, thrived in an age when few—men, women, boys, or girls—left home without a hat. I am old enough to remember the excitement of receiving my new Easter bonnet each year. Who can forget the Gainsborough hats worn at the Ascot race in *My Fair Lady* or the cloches common in the era of *The Great Gatsby*? Hats were a necessity and a statement of fashion until the 1960s, when their popularity just wore out. Fancy hats are no more.

This is a story of history and cultural changes. But more important, it is a story of the personal strength of one woman and her survival during tough times. Through her community commitment, she epitomizes the meaning of shared life together that has relevance for all of us.

I came to Annapolis in 1958 when Mrs. Musterman's hat shop at 197 Main Street was still thriving. By reputation I knew this was a special store in our city. And Mrs. Musterman also happened to be the grandmother of my good friend and classmate at Towson High School, the talented Peggy Houghton (née Musterman). I would walk by L.P. Musterman's hat shop window, but I never went inside and introduced myself as a friend of her granddaughter. My loss.

Now through Elizabeth's book I have met Lillian Musterman, a woman with a smile and a generous friendly nature. I learned that Mrs. Musterman's wisdom benefitted old and young and just about everyone who met her. Annapolis also benefitted from the author's role in founding what is now the Annapolis Maritime Museum. For this contribution I was happy to honor her with a citation when I was mayor.

In 1971, at age ninety, Lillian was honored by the Annapolis chapter of Zonta, the "women's Rotary," of which she was a charter member. This organization seeks to empower women. Pictures of her were shown as tales of her life were shared. The moderator closed the celebration with: "Musty, yours has been an amazing life, full of love and laughter, sorrow and joy, ambition and its fulfillment, difficulties, experience, and the love and admiration of many more people than you may realize."

This book is a must read for anyone interested in what makes ordinary people like Mrs. Musterman so special to the goodness of our lives and community.

Ellen Moyer, Mayor of Annapolis, 2001–2009

PREFACE

THIS BIOGRAPHY IS A story of one twentieth-century woman—Lillian Powell Musterman (née Johnson). An ordinary woman, she would be loath to name herself a feminist, although she opened a hat shop in Annapolis, Maryland, alone as the Roaring Twenties dawned, and she was still greeting customers as the Women's Movement of the 1960s took off. Her working life spanned the first sixty-seven years of the 1900s—all as a milliner. Few people are milliners today and even fewer know what the word means: artistic creator of hats. Yes. Hats were her business and with hats she supported her family.

This woman, who faced challenges with sheer grit and tenacity, met them, and moved on, was my grandmother. My women cousins and I all agree that she was our inspiration as we traveled through the rough patches of our lives. Our Gran could do it, had done it, and so we could too.

Since her death, I've pored through her picture album, collection of newspaper clippings, and carefully saved letters; walked through the house where she bore her children; shopped in the store she once owned. Her childhood town of

Onancock in Virginia calls to me. I've traveled there many times to walk the streets and remember the summer when I was a teenager and strolled them with her. She told me stories about her early life as she pointed out her church, her home, her parents' graves. On my first trip as an adult, I found the cemetery and the tales came flooding back. Then it came to me. When I'm gone, no one will know anything about her. Not my children or grandchildren. Not the Mustermans of Annapolis or Annapolitans themselves. I had to write her story.

If I chose to limit this book to my memories of my grandmother, I could not adequately honor her life. Lillian Musterman was more than my reminiscences. I began to search for what that "more" was. Member of the business community, creative milliner and seamstress, churchgoer, entrepreneur, friend to many, kind to all. Her story of joy and loss, struggle and success, and challenges met with grace speaks to women everywhere. She once stated her philosophy: "Nothing is impossible if you really want to do it."

As I researched this book, I felt it was my chance to collect family tales and legends in one place and sneak in bits about Annapolis as well. I hope that my love for this woman, the Musterman family, and the town are evident. As you read along, enjoy wandering down Main Street and looking in at the hats in L.P. Musterman Hat Shop. Step in and try on a few. And go upstairs. Visit the family living above the store. Learn about this independent woman of the early twentieth century; about how she and other milliners apprenticed and ran their businesses; and how a woman with talent, courage, and determination lived out her life in a small town.

1

AT MRS. MUSTERMAN'S HAT SHOP

O N A BRISK MARCH day, just when spring was in the air, women bustled up Main Street with excitement, anticipation, and expectation. They were heading to Mrs. Musterman's hat shop. For more than forty years—from the 1920s to the late 1960s—L.P. Musterman's was known as the "most elite hat shop" in Annapolis, Maryland.[1] Teenagers going to next Saturday's tea fight at the Naval Academy[2] arrived at the door giggling with their friends. Little girls hoping to find a new spring bonnet held their mothers' hands as they approached the shop.

At the window, on the edge of the broad display shelf among her hats, sat Mrs. Musterman. As each customer opened the door at 197 Main Street, she rose in greeting, the bell tinkling as the door opened and shut.

Mrs. Musterman was known for her welcoming nature, her chuckle, her kind approach. She spoke with a soft southern drawl, revealing to some that she was from the Eastern Shore of Virginia. She stood about five foot four, was plump and round, and opened her arms wide to greet friends and family. Those lucky enough to get a hug were surprised when they felt a stiffness as their arms encircled her—her whale-bone corset. As they snuggled in, they caught a whiff of rose-water scent.

Every day found her in a simple dress of linen, cotton, or rayon with a thin belt at the waist. She chose dark and muted colors, often with a print. Her hem discreetly below her knee. On her feet were clunky-heeled, lace-up shoes—black in fall and winter, white in spring and summer. Her jewelry was simple too: one day a cameo brooch with earrings to match, a string of pearls the next. Sometimes a pin of gold leaves and seed pearl grapes graced her lapel. Mrs. Musterman's hair went from brown to gray to white over the years and from marcelled waves[3] to straight. She pulled it back in a tidy bun pinned at the back of her head. Plain-framed glasses complemented her round face. Her skin, pure as fresh cream, not once was touched by makeup. It seemed she didn't wrinkle as she aged, and she never lost the twinkle in her eye.

Each spring and fall Mrs. Musterman filled her store with new hats fresh from New York and Baltimore for the season "openings." Customers were surrounded by reds and pinks, blues and purples, blacks and tans. Hats covered the counters, rested on shelves, and perched on metal stands. Some were straw, some cloth. A few were made of felt, others covered in feathers. Their brims ranged from large to small, upturned to slanted down, stiff to floppy to none at all. Veiling, silk flowers, and berries lay in the glass cases ready for embellishing or brightening up a hat. Young girls spun on the polished floor as their mothers decided what to try first.

Sometimes a boy was dragged along by a grandmother, but he didn't last long. Boys would hover near the glass-framed door for a bit, then sneak outside when no one was looking. They might go to the candy store next door before crossing the street, sucking a red hot ball as they headed for the pawn shop (now Back Creek Books). Under the "Public Loan Office" sign, they gazed in the window at the knife display. It seemed those knives never changed. Down Main Street the boy would wander farther away to Woolworth's to buy a squirt gun before stopping at Read's Drugstore to page through the comic books. There he'd read on the sly until his grandmother arrived with hat box in hand. As they headed to a booth at the back, he spun the red stools at the lunch counter. Once settled, they ordered Read's special deluxe hamburger.

Back at the hat shop, young girls and women were sampling the current styles. Fifty years later customers recalled the delight of being there: "Such a beautiful shop." Or Mrs. Musterman herself: "Awesome lady" with "the beautiful hats." Many young ladies from the 1920s to the 1960s bought their wedding going-away hats at the hat shop. Even a cross-dresser remembers buying his hats at Musterman's. (Did Mrs. Musterman suspect?)

Hats weren't the only items Mrs. Musterman trimmed, altered, and sold. A niece found Barbie doll clothes and a silk scarf bordered with mink under the Christmas tree one year. Another little girl slipped her hands into a favorite muff and wore the matching felt hat trimmed in fox fur. A gift from her mother that she still cherishes today. All were fashioned by Mrs. Musterman.[4]

Helping women select the right hat from her vast assortment was Mrs. Musterman's pleasure every day. As she walked across the floor to a customer, she might say, "Try this—it will flatter your oval face." Some ladies arrived following lunch with neighbors at the Capital Restaurant across the street or after a phosphate or soda when that building held Muhlmeister's Ice Cream Parlor. A friend might hold high a hanger, unveil a dress, and say "Musty, I'd like to match this. I just bought it at the Anita Shop." Or a niece would open a shoe box from Lipman's Bootery or Snyder's and show off her new shiny pink shoes and say, "Aunt Lil, can you find me a hat to go with these?"

Mrs. Musterman didn't work alone in her store. She was assisted through the early years by Mrs. Kashner, and in the later years by Mrs. Zang. Together these ladies helped customers consider and choose hats. One might encourage, "With such beautiful long hair as yours, a hat like this will work best—and see how it looks if you put your hair up." Or the other might say, "Let me add a little veiling here to soften the brim." And turning to another customer with another hat to try, Mrs. Musterman would encourage, "This one will favor your eyes." The women paid attention if they heard "No, not *that* one." Mrs. Musterman never hesitated when she believed a hat didn't suit and would never let a customer leave the store with a hat that "wouldn't do."

Once a woman found a hat to consider, she crossed the store, sat on the velvet-covered stool and preened in front of the antique diamond-dust mirror. Her image was framed in gilt Rococo molding that had ornate curlicues arching over at the top, almost touching the ceiling. As a customer considered, she adjusted the hat back, forward, akimbo, then reached for the hand mirror to check the look from behind. If not quite satisfied, she returned the hat to its stand and looked for another.

Mrs. Musterman didn't stock hats specifically made for little girls, but often the small-brimmed adult hats worked just as well. Sometimes she simply added some stiff veiling and bright flowers to last year's bonnet until it looked brand new. But, if that didn't please the girl, she'd make a hat from scratch. Whether they found a hat or not, the girls had fun following their mothers around the store and trying on all the merchandise.

The ladies of Annapolis could spend an hour or more as they considered 'most every hat in the store. While they did, Mrs. Musterman asked about their family or where they vacationed that summer. Sometimes it seemed more like visiting than shopping. Once the perfect hat was selected, Mrs. Musterman wrapped it in tissue paper, put it in a hexagonal cardboard box, placed the cover, and tied a bow on top. Out the door the customer went, proudly carrying her maroon box with the pink lid stamped "L.P. Musterman Hat Shop."

.

2

LIL THE COUNTRY GIRL

*M*ANY CUSTOMERS NOTICED MRS. Musterman's southern lilt when she spoke, and some probably guessed she was from Virginia. But none could imagine her as a little girl in the 1880s running through rows of corn with her sister Nan. Lil—that was her nickname—and her family lived in a little house next to her grandfather's farm house. His cornfields were behind the two houses.

"We would go out in Grandfather Johnson's cornfield when he was away and steal ears of corn and strip the husks off and make our doll babies. Then we'd dress them up."

Lil and Nan stripped the ears of corn, folded the moist corn husks, and tied a string at the top for the doll's head and a string in the middle for a waist. They rolled a narrow strip of husk to make arms and hands and slipped it through the body. Once the husks dried, they gave their doll babies—they always called them doll babies—a smile with an ink pen. They probably rummaged through their mother's sewing basket for cloth and ribbons to make doll clothes. Lil's mother taught the girls early to protect a finger with a thimble and to make just about anything with a needle and thread. Lil was on her way to becoming a seamstress. It would take longer to become a milliner.

~

The woman some thought of as the "Hat Lady on Main Street" was named Lillian Powell Johnson on the chilly day of her birth, December 8, 1881. The Johnson family lived in Onancock,[1] Virginia, a sleepy southern town on Virginia's Eastern Shore, which was still recovering from the Civil War.

Lillian was the fifth and youngest child in her family. Her siblings were Abbie Rose, George Thomas, Hezekiah Newton, and Margaret Nancy. Her father, George Washington Johnson, was a waterman. He earned the title Captain by sailing the Chesapeake Bay oystering and hauling produce and other goods. Her mother, Margaret Anne FitzGerald Johnson, was a seamstress and a dressmaker. Although she had never attended school, she could read and write and was a constant correspondent with distant family members. At least one of Lillian's aunts was a milliner.

The many relatives who lived near or in Onancock carried the names of Crockett, Hopkins, FitzGerald, Johnson, and Powell.[2] All were descended from English and Irish colonists. Her earliest known ancestor, Robert Hopkins, arrived in the Maryland colony in the late 1600s. One hundred years later, Stephen Hopkins settled on Smith Island, Maryland. John Crockett was the first constable on Tangier Island, Virginia, in the early 1700s. Two generations later, Stephen A. Hopkins, the son of Leah Crockett and Stephen Hopkins, crossed the Chesapeake Bay from Smith Island to open a store in Onancock in the early 1800s.

Stephen A. Hopkins' sons were ambitious, active in the

community, and economically comfortable. One was Onancock's first mayor; two others were councilmen; and another served as the first president of the Onancock National
Bank, which was founded in his living room. Generations of
the family ran the Hopkins & Bro. Store at the town wharf
from before its incorporation in 1842 until 1966. That year,
the Eastern Shore of Virginia Historical Society bought the
building to preserve the original exterior and store cabinetry
and now exhibits general store artifacts and a display of the
building's history.[3]

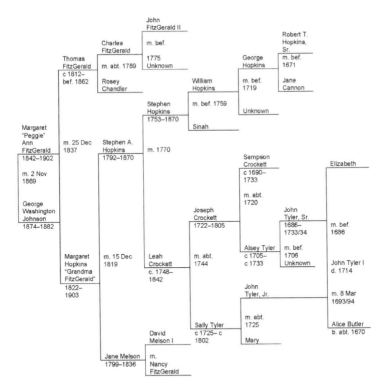

Direct Ancestors of Lillian Powell Johnson's Mother
Margaret "Peggie" Anne FitzGerald

The wharf in Onancock was a hub of activity year round. Watermen loaded their sailing skiffs with Eastern Shore produce to deliver to cities up and down the Bay in the summer. In 1882, the local paper, the *Peninsula Enterprise,* reported "a thousand barrels or more of peas and about five-hundred crates of berries were shipped from Onancock to Baltimore …[4]

When Lil was a girl, townfolk went to Hopkins Wharf to shop at the store, pick up their mail, and board steamboats for Baltimore, Hampton, and other towns on the Bay. Today visitors go there to eat at the restaurant or climb aboard a boat for a day on Tangier Island. Tourists stroll along the streets of Onancock among white antebellum homes, shops, and restaurants, many with the same hammered tin ceilings that Lil saw when she shopped in town.

Her grandfather Johnson, "Cap'n Tom," had forebears dating back to before the Revolution too. At one time he was a Civil War blockade runner and while Lil was a girl, was reported to own more property in Accomack County than any other person. He tonged for oysters into his eighties and died in his nineties after falling from a buggy. He'd been out with a lady friend (not his wife) when a clap of thunder made the horse rear up, it's been said.[5] Lil inherited some of that spunk and ambition but was always the proper lady.

Lil's father, Cap'n George, plied the waters of the Chesapeake Bay in his "canoe," as many who sailed boats made of hollow logs called their boats. [6] It was either a bugeye or a pungy, both graceful sailing vessels with clipper bowsprits and two raked masts.[7]

From September through December, he and his crew dredged for oysters. In summer, they hauled produce up and down the Chesapeake Bay. When his canoe was empty, he loaded it with oyster shells to deliver to towns wanting to cover their dirt streets—which most did once a year.

Working the water was how Lil's father supported his growing family. But eight days before Christmas in 1882, dreadful news arrived at the Johnson home: Cap'n George had drowned. Tragedy struck as he headed home from Baltimore in a fierce storm on the Bay. He never made shore. Lil's mother clutched her baby close to her breast as she and the children stood at the graveside. Cap'n George's friends read Masonic honors and the Methodist minister said the prayers. It was December 20, 1882. Now the young family was thrown into poverty.

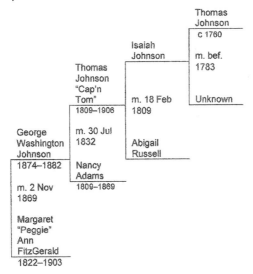

Direct Ancestors of Lillian Powell Johnson's Father
George Washington Johnson

Years later, after she moved from the Eastern Shore, Lil returned often to Onancock. It was not just to visit family, she also paid her respects to the father she never knew. At his gravesite on Hill Street, she brought out clippers to clear the grass away from the base of his marker and gazed at the carved sailing vessel above his name. His stone fell flat to the ground in the 1990s, and grass encroaches, trying to cover it. Today when a granddaughter comes to pay her respects, she too brings clippers plus a knife to remove the grass growing around and over the stone. She cleans the marker so the clipper's billowing sails are visible again.

Lil's nieces said that her mother "went to pieces" when she heard the news of her husband's drowning.[8] And so did Lil's oldest sister Abbie. Just ten years old at the time, Abbie became so nervous she had to stay home from school because of her involuntary writhings, which the doctor misdiagnosed as St. Vitus Dance. Lil's grandfather—Cap'n Tom—stepped in to help. He built the family a small house next to his and supported them in other ways when needed.[9]

The new widow, Lil's mother Peggie Johnson, took in sewing as her mother had when she was widowed early in the Civil War. Lil's two brothers, George and Hezzie, were put to work on their grandfather Johnson's farm. He also taught them to sail skiffs and tong for oysters. The girls—Abbie, Nan, and Lil—learned to bake bread and cakes; make apple sauce and pies; steam crabs and oysters; fry crab cakes and chicken; feed the chickens and gather eggs; milk the cow; plant and harvest the vegetables; make, mend, and wash the clothes; and trim their bonnets. The family survived.

After dinner on a hot summer's day, Lil's mother would say: "Now, Lil, gather up the leftovers and take them to the well." Lil cleared the butter, milk, and cream from the table and put them into a metal milk box together with any leftover food. She carried the box out back of the house to the well and lowered it into the coolness below so nothing soured. Lil didn't like this job. "Every time I leaned over the sides of the well, I was always afraid I'd fall in. Whenever I looked down, I felt that way. But I never told my mother. Of course she would have had one of the other children do it if she'd known. I never got over it."[10]

Sometimes in the late afternoon, it's likely her mother said: "Lil, it's time to go find the cow and bring her in for milking." Lil didn't like this job either, but out she went to the fields behind the house to search. When she finally found the cow, she had to make the stubborn beast come home with her. "I just hated bringing that cow home in the evening,"[11] she said. But Lil didn't complain. She was such a good little girl that she remembered being spanked only once, when she ran away to the tenant's home on her grandfather's land to play with their children.[12]

From her house on Holly Street to the wharf was less than a mile. Everything Lil did happened in between. Attending Sunday school. Going to school. Visiting her aunts and uncles, cousins, and Grandmother FitzGerald.

On a spring day, Lil would walk to town on the rutted country road of dust and dirt that turned to glistening white from a fresh topping of oyster shells near the shops. She'd hear the soft clip clop of hooves as donkeys and horses pulled carts full of potatoes and yams to the wharf. The sound changed to crunches when the hooves and steel tires met the hard-packed shells. She stepped up onto the wooden sidewalk in front of the stores, glad her hand-me-down shoes were safe from the sharp shells that could scrape and tear the leather.

Beyond the stores were the town square, Cokesbury Methodist Church, and large white homes with broad porches surrounded by expansive lawns on both sides of Market Street. An aunt or uncle would wave from the door and give her a shout hello or her cousin Virginia Hopkins might ask her to play on the porch at "The Beeches." (Locals still call it Hopkins House.)[13]

At the end of Market Street, she'd go into Hopkins & Bro. Store on the wharf to pick up the mail or purchase something her mother needed. She'd stay awhile and chat with her uncle Charlie FitzGerald, a clerk there.

Some days Lil climbed the hill across from the wharf to visit her Aunt Lysha.[14] She often found her shelling peas in a little alcove, where a breeze from the creek cooled them on a hot day.[15]

On other days she visited with her Grandma FitzGerald. Her house was half-way between Lil's home and the wharf, across from the town square on King Street. Known as the FitzGerald House, it was built in the traditional Eastern Shore style of "big house, little house, colonnade, and kitchen."[16] There Lil sat on the floor by Grandma FitzGerald's knee as she creaked back and forth in her rush-bottomed, ladder-backed rocking chair. Years later she described her visits:[17]

Sometimes they'd bring her beans, and she'd sit in that little rocker and break them. My Aunt Sallie did the cooking and there was always plenty of food. It was like another world. Grandma FitzGerald would tell me stories of the Civil War and how the Union soldiers came into the house [their home either in or near Hampton, Virginia] and bayoneted the beds in case a man was hiding in there. When they [the soldiers] left, the women went to the yard, where my mother held the lantern high while Grandma Fitz-Gerald sewed up the pigs after the Yankees cut them with their sabers. They hoped to deprive the Southerners of food, but some of those pigs did live.

Lil listened as Grandma FitzGerald told about crossing the Chesapeake with twelve children early in the Civil War. Her brother sent one of his sloops over to Virginia to bring his newly widowed sister and her children back across the Bay to safety on the Shore. Grandma FitzGerald brought out treasured letters so Lil could read what her uncle Nimmie (Nehemiah FitzGerald) had written about the Civil War battles he fought in and later about California, where he taught school after the war ended.[18]

More than 150 years after that war, the rush-bottomed rocker is still in the family and has rocked many a mother and baby to sleep. Although the chair has no arms, no one has ever pitched out or dropped a baby to the floor.

Lil's favorite aunt was Margaret Johnson Powell, who lived in the eighteenth century Ker Place, a perfect example of Federal-period Georgian architecture and worth a visit today.[19] "I was given the middle name 'Powell' for Aunt Margaret. I spent many nights there—I was a special of hers."[20]

Lil went to Sunday school and other events at Cokesbury Methodist Church—not the newer Methodist Church, South,

15

founded during the Civil War. A favorite event was taffy pulling—their "main get-together. We'd burn our hands." Her great-great grandmother (Leah Crockett Hopkins) was buried in the churchyard, and Lil knew where the gravesite was—or had been. On her later visits when she brought her family to Onancock, she would point to a large tree that had grown right through the grave, saying, "That is where Leah Crockett is buried." The tree survived for more than 100 years.[21]

Lil did everything with Nan, her older sister by eighteen months. They played and argued and teased. To dress up for Sunday school, they'd add a ribbon to their everyday clothes. "You would wind a ribbon around your neck and tie a bow. And then, if you wanted it for a sash, you could put your arms through and bring it down." Lil's sister Nan, flamboyant and strong willed, some have said, was always up to something or pestering someone. "She used to take my things and wear them. I'd have a ribbon around my waist, and Nan would get it away from me. I chased her home many a time for taking something of mine." Just like sisters.[22]

Young Lil completed only grades one through eight—all the free schooling provided by Virginia when she was a girl. Her first years were in a one-room schoolhouse and the last were in the new school (built in 1894) with four classrooms. It was known as one of the best and largest schools on the Eastern Shore of Virginia at the time. There the boys played jokes on the girls, like pulling their hair and running away.

Mr. Joynes, our principal, [would] say, "We're going to sleigh ride tonight." The hill was in the schoolyard. Mama would let us go because she knew that he would look after us. We'd have sometimes ten to twenty-five children, and he'd see that too many didn't go at one time. On Saturdays, we'd go to the woods. He'd make a fire, and we'd take shasters [clusters of long pine needles] to line the fire. Then we'd roast sweet potatoes and apples.[23]

Lil never forgot the year of "the big snow"—probably the March 1888 blizzard known as the Great White Hurricane. One of the neighbors had a "wonderful big sleigh" and gave rides to everyone. "The snow was so deep that year," she said, "you could walk along the tops of the fence posts."

"When we two girls [Nan and Lil] got old enough, [our] sister Abbie gave each of us one earring." These were special earrings. Their mother had given them to Abbie when their father died in 1882, twelve years before. "Nan wanted this other earring in the worst way. She offered me everything. 'Lil, how about my doll crib?' And when she offered that, I finally gave in and gave her my earring for the doll crib."[24]

Before she left Onancock, Lil did have one early romance. She and her young fellow went on "a buggy ride about town." Do you think she got a kiss at the end of that ride? "My lan's, no! We didn't do things like that."[25]

Lil's siblings began leaving Onancock when she was a teenager. Her brother Hezzie, who never got along with Grandfather Johnson, set out on his own as soon as he was of age. Next Abbie—swept off her feet by a young carpenter come down from Salisbury to help build a house in town. Nan left for Baltimore to become a milliner. Only her brother, George, who eventually inherited their grandfather Johnson's farm, remained. When she was sixteen or seventeen it was her turn. Her mother and her uncles and aunts and cousins and friends bid her goodbye and good luck.

Although Lil left Onancock, the people never left her heart. For all the years of her life, she returned to visit with her children and grandchildren. She introduced them to relatives, showed them the family homes, visited the gravesites, and told stories about growing up in a small town.

3

YOUNG LIL BECOMES A MILLINER

*O*FF SHE WENT, THIS young woman, this Lillian Powell Johnson from Onancock, Virginia, to become a
milliner.[1] She had her clothes and hats, a goal, and
determination.

She probably took a steamboat, or perhaps a train, to
Salisbury, Maryland. She lived there with her sister Abbie.
Most likely her skills as a seamstress allowed her to pay for
her keep. But she didn't stay long. On she moved to the noise,
traffic, and opportunity of Baltimore—and her sister Nan. Lil
found a room at the YWCA, where meals and a safe residence
were available to the young women who flooded to the city in
search of jobs. Some residents became her life-long friends.

Nan was working as a milliner for Armstrong, Cator &
Co.,[2] a flourishing millinery. Its ads appeared monthly in *The
Illustrated Milliner* listed under "Importers, Jobbers, Manu-
facturers." But Armstrong Cator was a retailer as well as a
wholesaler of millinery goods and notions. And the company
apprenticed milliners for itself and other establishments all
over the country. Olive Ann Burns described how the system
worked in her 1984 novel *Cold Sassy Tree*:

Grandpa was real proud of the store's having a milliner trained at Armstrong, Cator & Company. In 1901, the company had sent Miss Love and her friend out to a big store in Texas. When she wanted to leave Texas, Armstrong Cator sent her, sight unseen, to Grandpa [in Georgia].[3]

~

Nan probably took Lil to Armstrong Cator for an interview. The two wore long skirts, big hats, and gloves, and perhaps they carried a parasol to protect their fair skin from the sun. Buildings stretched five, six, seven, even ten stories high. Carriages and carts clattered and clicked along. Occasionally a motor car rumbled by.

When the sisters arrived at Armstrong Cator, they certainly peered up at the five-story building towering above them. Each floor had six pillared archways framing the windows. Down the street were more buildings for manufacturing: a foundry for producing hat blocks, a building devoted to sizing and dyeing, and a large shipping facility. Another entire building was used for blocking hats cut from flat felt.

As Nan pointed at the façade of brick and windows she said: "That floor is all ready-to-wear trimmed hats. That one tailored hats." The next might hold ribbons, artificial flowers, nuts, and—until the Migratory Bird Act was passed in 1918—wild bird feathers of many varieties and brilliant colors.[4] Silks and velvets on another level. Veils and veiling would have a whole floor. So would braids, tassels, and heavy embroidery. "You'll find buyers and milliners on the top floors examining wholesale products and placing their orders."

Everything a milliner needed was available at Armstrong Cator. Even the milliners.

"The trimming room," said Nan, "is the very top floor." Lil gazed at the windows and imagined the bevy of activity as hundreds of milliners worked on that floor. Copying hats. Learning the latest trims for the new season. Adding veils and flowers and feathers. That was the floor Lil wanted. That was why she had come to Baltimore.

The sisters passed through the imposing entrance to a large public reception space on the ground floor. Its seating areas were filled with ladies resting, perhaps waiting for a friend to join them, before visiting the grand salon. In the salon, velvet settees reflected by gilt mirrors lined the walls. Chairs with tasseled fringe were placed around low tables. Customers viewed the display of model hats on brass stands and picked one or two to be copied for the new season. Buyers and visiting milliners would go right on through these customer waiting rooms to the floors holding wholesale merchandise.

Nan and Lillian walked right through, too.

Nan had completed her two-year apprenticeship and was traveling for Armstrong Cator. Now it was Lil's turn. Up they went to the general offices and straight to Mr. Wiler's door. He was the Armstrong Cator representative who filled requests for milliners from stores throughout the United States. Some assignments lasted a few weeks, some a lifetime.

When he called them in, Nan surely introduced Lil to Mr. Wiler, "My sister has come to be a milliner and her fine skills as a seamstress are as good as mine. In fact, we both learned at our mother's knee."

But that first day ended in disappointment. Lil was

assigned to the retail store itself. There she waited on ladies as they looked through bandboxes of millinery and notions. She helped customers find the perfect trimmings for their hats. She suggested ready-made hats to ladies looking for a quick, economical purchase. As Lil stood behind a customer seated at a large mirror, she held a hand mirror so the lady could see all around a grand Gainsborough hat. Lil might tilt the hat slightly for a better angle or suggest a veil, maybe a feather. Those elaborate, wide-brimmed hats had been in vogue since the 1700s, when the artist Thomas Gainsborough immortalized them. Also called picture hats, these creations were piled high with feathers, furs, flowers, fruits, and nuts. They were all the rage as the nineteenth century turned to the twentieth. Especially the hats trimmed with feathers. Even a whole bird, maybe two.[5]

~

Now eighteen, young Lil was an accomplished seamstress, and although she had no millinery experience, she was confident about her skills. After three weeks on the retail floor, she gathered up her courage and went to Mr. Wiler.[6] This time alone. She didn't care where he sent her. She just knew that she wanted to create hats, not only sell them. She told this story many times:

> Mr. Wiler said, "Miss Johnson, tell me what you know and what you don't so that I can understand how you believe that you are a milliner." I thought, I can't tell him that I know much because I've only been here two weeks. I think he likes me because I don't brag on myself.

Perhaps she brought him a sample of her work or explained a particularly difficult millinery task. Whatever she did or said convinced Mr. Wiler. Before the day ended, Lillian took her place among the women in the workroom of one of the millincies.[7] Together with the other milliners she trimmed the hats and sent them down to the store.

Lillian joined the other young ladies around a worktable covered with thimbles, scissors of various types, tape measures, tailor's chalk, pins, and needles—long and short, thick and thin. A pressing board was nearby. Irons sat atop small stands, heating over a flame fueled by butane. A kettle simmered on a hot plate ready to steam a wrinkled veil. Pressing cushions of many configurations to match all possible head sizes and shapes were scattered about. Treadle sewing machines lined the walls.

Some young ladies sat at machines creating hats from scratch. Feet pumped treadles, which set off a whirl of wheels driving needles up and down, up and down. Deft hands guided fabric under the needles. Other young women stood at tables lined with hat blocks or forms—some wooden, some iron. On each block was an unadorned hat base: fabric layered and stretched over a rigid core of starched linen or muslin or buckram.[8] Concealed within the base was the hat's skeleton—an iron wire frame three to five inches high that helped to hold the hat's shape. "Careful of those," an experienced milliner probably cautioned as Lil twisted iron wire. "Too many pricks and you'll die of blood poisoning."

Sometimes the hat assigned to a milliner was not new, but rather one a customer sent each season to be stripped to its base and redesigned with the latest notions. The milliner removed all the old trim and set the base on the work table.

She paused. She pondered. She turned it this way and that. Aha. She was ready to transform the old form. As she worked, something grand emerged.

If the hat needed a new cover, the milliner went to work cutting fabric to fit the shape—crown tip, sideband, and brim. Sometimes nimble fingers glued fabric over the frame. Other times a milliner took up a heavy-duty straight needle, threaded it with millinery thread, donned a thimble, and worked the needle back and forth through all the layers.

The milliners swished back and forth, hems brushing across the floor. Their long skirts rustled as they went from work tables to shelves to drawers. They chose feathers, flowers, and fruits. Veils, ruffles, and ribbons. Beadwork and braid. Cords and tassels of silver and gold. They piled decorations so high that often the shape of the hat itself disappeared. They stepped back, looked, leaned forward, and added one more item. Finally another plain base was transformed into a crown worthy of Sunday church services or afternoon tea.

It took Lil just one week to prove her skill and competence on the trimming floor. Mr. Wiler sent her off to Whitestone, Virginia—her first assignment. Thus ended what must have been the shortest millinery apprenticeship on record.

The small town of Whitestone in the Northern Neck of Virginia sits on the water where the Rappahannock River meets the Chesapeake Bay. It is almost directly across the Bay from where Lil grew up. Perhaps she looked up some relatives who had moved there following the Civil War. Maybe she boarded a steamboat to cross the Bay and visit her mother.

Her next assignments took her to the mountains of Western Maryland: first Frostburg, then Cumberland. Each time she left Baltimore, Lil said goodbye to Nan and the other milliners and headed for the train station with anticipation mixed with anxiety about what awaited her. She made friends each place she went, both in the millincies where she worked and the houses where she boarded. On their days off, she and her friends would picnic in the mountains or walk to the shops in the city and attend band concerts in the town square.

Winters in hilly Appalachia were frigid, and in the first years of the new century, central heating, even in the large cities, rarely warmed a boarder's room. Lillian may have felt a tinge of claustrophobia walking up and down the steep streets lined with gray, stone buildings in these cold mountain towns. She must have sorely missed the fields and woods of the Eastern Shore and the waters of the Chesapeake Bay.

Between her assignments, Lil returned to Baltimore, renewed friendships, and took her place among the ladies on the trimming floor of Armstrong Cator. The milliners worked together as they waited for the next opportunity. One day a girl interrupted Lil just as she was finishing a hat. "Miss Johnson, Mr. Wiler wants to see you."

Lillian went down to his office.

Mr. Wiler said "I think I have a position for you. Stick around."

But because Lil had a date to go shopping with Nan, she left when her work was done. She knew better than to keep her feisty sister waiting. Just as she stepped through the door at the YWCA, a messenger arrived. "Return," he said.

Lil rode the streetcar back to Armstrong Cator's and took a seat on the "mourner's bench." Nervous young milliners would sit on this long bench for hours outside the interview room, awaiting their turn. Each one hoped a millinery job would be the reward. As one was called in for an interview, the others slid up the bench, getting closer to the door. Each young lady entered the interview room alone to be looked over and hired or rejected. A store owner needing a milliner would pick the one deemed most suitable. Years later, when relating this story, Lillian said that it always reminded her of buying horses.

Mr. Wiler told Lil that the lady wanting to meet her was still out, but expected momentarily. She recalled:

> I wasn't one for waiting and didn't see how anyone could sit there, but I did it. For a while. But I left again after an hour because she didn't come and didn't come. I had just gotten in the house again and there came a second messenger. "Come immediately!" he said.

Lil went back to Armstrong Cator, only to learn that this time the lady was out shopping and would return in half an hour. Mr. Wiler wanted no delay when she arrived, but knew that Lil might not stay for long. He said: "Would you sit on that bench there?"

"Yes," said Lil, "but I don't like it."

"But you're going to like it now. You're going to sit there until this lady comes in."

Fifteen minutes later a handsome, stylish woman swept through the outer room past the mourners' bench. Head held high, looking neither left nor right, she entered the interview room—the "inner sanctum," the milliners called it.

As the door closed, Lil thought, "I'm just a little ol' country girl who doesn't know anything. I never could work for her, all grand in her black dress and gloves and big black hat."

Mr. Wiler opened the door: "Thank the lands you stayed this time. Come on, someone wants to see you, and I think she's going to like you."

"That lady who just came in, she isn't for me, is she?"

"Yes, she is," Mr. Wiler said,

A nervous Lil, now almost twenty-two, was summoned inside and introduced to a formidable woman, Mrs. James Strange—Julia Maude Strange (née Higgins)—of Annapolis, Maryland. Mrs. Strange asked one question and one question only: "Can you fit velvet to buckram?"

Sewing velvet onto buckram is difficult to do well, but Lillian had done it.

"Yes," she said.

Mrs. Strange said, "I think you'll do."

Lil returned to her room at the YWCA to pack her trunk. As she folded her few dresses and boxed up her hats, she wondered, *How will I ever be able to satisfy such a smart-looking lady?*

4

LILLIAN ARRIVES IN ANNAPOLIS

*L*ILLIAN AND NAN SAT on a dark pew-like wooden bench in Baltimore's train station, chatting about the new century. They certainly had arrived plenty early, wore beautiful hats of their own design, and felt a hint of sadness mixed with excitement. Lillian was nervous about working for Mrs. Strange but full of hope about what was to come.

When the announcer called out the track number for Annapolis, they quickly turned to hug each other and exchange a peck on the cheek. Lillian scooped her skirt up in one hand, and toted her hand-grip and her purse in the other as she headed toward the train. She climbed the metal stairs to board the Baltimore and Annapolis Shortline Railroad. Her flat-top steamer trunk was in the baggage car with the total of her meager belongings. Today that trunk holds a great-grand-daughter's collection of stuffed bears. The B&A ran an hourly service between the two cities, so while it was goodbye, the sisters would visit each other often.

As the train chugged out of Baltimore, Lillian wondered what type of new life awaited her in the town some were calling the "Venice of the Chesapeake ... because of its eight bridges."[1] *How long will this assignment last? How long will I be in this town?* She probably never imagined then that Annapolis would be her home for the rest of her life.

Lillian found a window seat and waved to Nan, who got smaller and smaller as the train slowly pulled out of the station. Lillian settled in to view scenes of people in buggies waiting at the level crossings, heeding the shrill whistle as they watched the train go by. The train picked up speed as it left the city and was soon zipping along, clickety-clack, clickety-clack through the forests and fields.

The trip was not a long one, as those who have traveled between Annapolis and Baltimore know. Lillian rode a steam train, and the ride took thirty minutes. Later the trains were electric but the time to cover the distance was about the same. What never changed in the sixty years of the B&A service was the jerking and swaying of the cars as they moved along the tracks. Riders felt every jolt, joggle, and jiggle. No wonder they called the B&A "the Bump 'n Agony."

As the train swayed through the wooded countryside, Lillian heard the low, long whistle at the level crossings and the screech of brakes before stops along the way. Linthicum Heights. Earleigh Heights. Jumpers Hole. Round Bay. Jones Station. Arnold Station. After twenty minutes or so, the train slowed to barely a crawl. It had reached the Severn River.

Lillian peered down at the river below as the train crept across the long timber trestle bridge that spanned this wide body of water. She must have felt suspended above the river's swirling currents, although the bridge was not very high. Lillian would have sat perfectly still, not daring to move. Fearing that one slight shift of her weight—even an inch to the left or right—would plunge the train with all aboard into Severn River. Many who once rode that train remember the same fear during that crossing.[2]

Over the bridge, a stop in Wardour and another in West Annapolis, and all got dark as the train entered a covered bridge to cross College Creek. Daylight returned and the train slowed to a stop at Bladen Street station. She was in Annapolis. Lillian gathered up her bags and descended to the platform. She was ready to embrace her new life in the City of Annapolis.

Maryland's capital city was a bustling town, claiming almost ten thousand people in 1900. It had the Naval Academy, St. John's College, state and county governments, a sheltered harbor on the Chesapeake Bay, and businesses to support them all. The town had been building, improving, and modernizing for the past twenty years to be ready for the new century.

Lillian alighted to the platform at Bladen Street and hailed Mrs. Strange. Together they walked the few blocks to 194 Prince George Street, where Mrs. Strange had arranged boarding for her new employee. Lillian paused to gasp at the beauty of what architectural historians call an "exceptional Italianate town home."[3] Mrs. Strange climbed the few marble steps to rap the knocker on the heavily carved wood double door. Mrs. Brewer welcomed them in.

Lillian quickly learned that she would not be lonely there. The three-story structure was home not only to a widow, Mrs. Brewer (née Feldmeyer); her two daughters Marjorie and Dorothy; but also to her sisters, the Misses Feldmeyer—Emma S.,

Katherine, and Janie E., the last of whom never married.[4] One of their bachelor brothers may have been living there too—most likely the pharmacist James D. Feldmeyer.[5]

Once settled, Lillian went right to work. Six days a week, she arose, dressed, put on her hat, and stepped out the door—perhaps with her parasol in hand—to walk the several blocks to Mrs. Strange's shop at 205 Main Street.[6] J. M. Strange's was one of six millineries listed in the 1910 *Annapolis City Directory*—four of them on Main Street. In the early 1900s, most shops were open from 7 a.m. to 9:30 p.m., Monday through Friday, except Wednesdays. The busiest day was Saturday, when they didn't close until midnight.[7]

As Lillian stepped out the front door, she would have noticed the construction going on next door as the once grand colonial Paca House was being converted to the Carvel Hall Hotel.[8] She headed up Prince George Street, passing old brick homes, some Victorian and some colonial, with iron boot scrapers on the sidewalks at the foot of their stairs. At Maryland Avenue she turned left and saw the white wooden dome of the Maryland State House in the distance on State Circle.[9] Stores and homes lined the avenue. In the middle of the block was one of the many public water pumps that citizens without inside plumbing relied on. She continued to State Circle; the State House was now on the hill to her right. At the corner of East Street was Gilbert's Pharmacy, and between East and Cornhill streets was the Circle Theatre; both are restaurants today. She passed another public water pump at Francis Street in front of the Bond Hotel. When she reached the side of State Circle that was opposite from where she had entered, she turned left to walk through Franklin's Alley (briefly called Chancery Lane) to upper Main Street. Her last steps took her across the cobblestones to Mrs. Strange's millinery at 205 Main Street.

As she looked up and down the street, store merchants were busy spreading their awnings across wood frames to show that they were open for business. Main Street was about half homes and half businesses when the 1900s began. By mid-century, all the structures were businesses, most with apartments above for shop owners and working class families.

Lillian arrived at Mrs. Strange's millinery and set to work. The shop was stocked with both ready-to-wear hats and buckram bases for custom-made hats. Lillian arranged newly trimmed hats in the storefront window to tempt customers on their way down Main Street. She waited on patrons and discussed ways to retrim an old hat in the latest style for the upcoming season. Recent editions of *The Milliner* and other fashion magazines were on hand to help customers choose a style and get ideas for adornment. She said:[10]

> We'd buy a few sports things [hats]. But the rest of the hats we made. In the wintertime, if I couldn't find a fur hat that suited [a customer], I'd show her a hat that she liked in the shop. I'd have the buckram, and I would imitate it. A custom-made hat began at three dollars for those big Gainsborough hats without trim. You had to have extra trimming for it. You made the hat with the ribbons. By the time I was finished with my work, the hat would cost about fifty or sixty dollars.[11]

It's been recorded that around 1900 some arrogant service personnel and Naval Academy professors thought of Annapolitans as provincial and remarked that "some women [of Annapolis] were said to not have bought a hat since Appomattox."[12] It's hard to imagine that to be true. Photographs collected by Marion Warren and his daughter Mame prove otherwise, especially those taken at Naval Academy festivities—the April 1906 internment of John Paul Jones' body in Bancroft Hall and the dedication of the Naval Academy Chapel doors during June Week 1909.[13] Certainly some of the women who appear bedecked in Gainsborough hats were Annapolitans and had purchased their hats at one of the town's six milliners: four on Main Street, including Mrs. Strange's; one on Maryland Avenue; and one on West Street.[14]

Although she was a boarder in the Feldmeyer's home, Lillian soon became a friend of the family. And Julia Strange turned out not to be so fearsome after all. In fact, she was a "delightful and thoughtful employer." Once when Lillian was sick, Julia brought Lillian to the Strange home to be cared for and recover.

Like Lillian, the Feldmeyers were Methodist. On Sundays, they dressed in their best, donned their hats, and walked together to the Methodist church—either the Wesley Chapel on the corner of Maryland Avenue and Prince George Street or Calvary Methodist Church on State Circle.[15]

The Feldmeyers always included Lillian in family activities. Fourth of July picnics across Spa Creek at the Feldmeyer farm in Eastport were big events, and she attended them for years. Members of the large family—there were at least eleven sisters and brothers altogether—came often to the house on Prince George Street to visit their sisters, and Lillian met them all. One was James, a bachelor. Another, John, was a pharmacist. But it was George,[16] a dentist, who came most often and brought his good friend, John Henry Musterman.[17]

When he met Lillian, John Henry was in his forties and thus far had escaped marriage. He had been born in Annapolis, the eldest son of German immigrants. At one time he was part owner of Gilbert's pharmacy on State Circle and later a clerk at the Naval Academy. He was a Knights Templar at the Annapolis Masonic Lodge and traveled to many states to attend their annual gatherings. How grand he must have looked in his uniform with gold epaulets, ceremonial sword, and "fore and aft" plumed hat for occasions at the Masonic Temple. He regularly attended dances and thrilled many a young woman when he signed his name on her dance card. He was known as "the most eligible bachelor in town."

Once Lillian and John Musterman met, his bachelor days were numbered. He was immediately taken with the smile and laughter of this demure and charming Virginia girl.

5

MISS JOHNSON BECOMES
MRS. MUSTERMAN

JOHN MUSTERMAN'S MANY NIECES went out of their
way to go up Main Street on their walk home from
school, hoping to catch a glimpse of the new young
lady their uncle was so crazy about. When they got to Mrs.
Strange's millinery, they lingered and peered into the shop
window. They knew their Uncle John was quite the dandy
around town, but to their knowledge he'd never had a lady
friend. And he was so old—over forty. Others also heard
about this new beauty in town. Eleanor Owings remembered
that when she was about fifteen, she and a girlfriend used to
slip by the millinery shop just to "peek at Lillian because she
was so pretty."[1]

It wasn't long before John Musterman and Lillian were
courting. Sometimes they went to see the "moving pictures"
on Main Street or State Circle. Other times they remained
at the Feldmeyers' home and visited with the family. They'd
walked down West Street or ride in a buggy to visit the various
Musterman and Westphal families in Annapolis. (John's sister
Elizabeth—Lizzie—had married John Westphal). Lillian said,

"He enjoyed being with his family, so we'd go [to their homes] and sit with them." Lillian became close friends with a niece of John's, Ruby Westphal (later Chaney).

Sometimes they traveled to Ocean City, a community of small cottages, five or six hotels, and a new fishing and recreation pier.[2] Lillian's oldest sister Abbie and her husband lived there in the summers. Other days off they took the train to Baltimore to visit her sister Nan who had married Frank Parsons in 1905. On Sundays after services, they strolled around the Naval Academy taking pictures of the new buildings of "imperial proportions" for her picture album.[3] A breezy day found them sailing in small craft on the Chesapeake Bay with friends.

After courting for several years, John and Lillian married on September 10, 1908.[4] She was twenty-six and he was forty-nine. The Eastern Shore paper, *The Peninsula Enterprise*, reported that the "quiet home ceremony" was held at her sister Nan's home at "Dukeland on the Bloomingdale Road, Walbrook, Baltimore." Miss Johnson arrived for the ceremony in her "traveling gown of dark blue broadcloth with hat and gloves to match." She carried a prayer book from which the ceremony was read. Nan, the only attendant, wore "white organdie [*sic*] and lace" and carried white roses. Following the Methodist ceremony, John and Lillian left on their wedding trip to Niagara Falls, Atlantic City, and other popular honeymoon destinations.[5]

Among the wedding gifts to the bride and groom was an elegant silver tea service that now sits on its large silver tray at a granddaughter's home. The tea pot is engraved "Compliments of ADA." Lillian never found out what ADA stood for: it was a secret society that included John Musterman, Dr. Feldmeyer, and several unknown others. Years later their daughter, Nancy Musterman, made up the name "the Annapolis Dudes Association," which is not hard to imagine when you see pictures of those men in high silk or derby hats. John Musterman also carried a monogrammed gold-headed cane, often wore spats, and always a tie. They were dandies for sure.

When the newlyweds returned from their wedding trip, they lived with the Feldmeyers in their home on Prince George Street. John returned to his job as a clerk at the Naval Academy, and the new Mrs. Musterman continued working in the millinery for Julia Strange.

She was not the only woman working in Annapolis. Her sister-in-law, Elizabeth Westphal, ran a candy store on the corner of Conduit and Union streets as had her mother, Anna Catherina Musterman (née Rehn), before her. Many of the corner greengrocers in Annapolis at the time were operated by women. The clerks in the larger groceries and dry goods stores were often women too. And the six millineries in Annapolis in 1910 were owned and staffed by women. Nationally, about twenty percent of women were in the labor force in 1910 and Lillian was one of them.

The couple socialized with Mrs. Strange and her son, Robert; with the Feldmeyers; and of course, with the Mustermans and the Westphals.

By their first anniversary, John and Lillian were busy looking for a place of their own. Annapolis was expanding and the newlyweds probably walked among the new housing sites beyond Cathedral Street all the way to the waters of Spa Creek. The lots ranged from some twelve to twenty-five feet wide and were intended for smaller houses—often duplexes—that served the merchant and middle classes. Some of the town's doctors bought several adjoining lots and built lovely homes with large sprawling lawns. These homes, conveniently near the hospital at Cathedral and South streets, were built with separate entrances for offices and examining rooms.

On their walk one day, John and Lillian may have turned onto Shaw Street and then up Dean Street. As they got close to Cathedral Avenue, they would have passed a row of small terraced houses being built. The houses had (and still have) cement stairs leading from the sidewalk up to a wide porch. Each had a small vestibule. Intrigued, the young couple went inside and found an entrance hall with a staircase to the second floor on the left and a doorway on the right into a sunny parlor. Toward the back of the house was a dining room and then the kitchen. A door from the kitchen led to a small yard. Lillian must have looked at the shiny glass-front cabinets and imagined her ruby and gold floral chinaware on the shelves.

Upstairs were three bedrooms and a bathroom with a claw-footed tub and small sink. Indoor plumbing. The attic space with its deep, slanted ceilings was large enough to house boarders to provide a bit of extra income. It was a house for a family.

John and Lillian arranged to rent the house at number 9 Dean Street and moved in after the New Year—1910. A year that held promises of a new home and their first child.

6

The Mustermans of Dean Street

*J*OHN AND LILLIAN COULDN'T have guessed the surprise in store for them. They had moved to the new home and settled in to await the birth of their first child. When the day arrived, February 4, 1910, Lillian gave birth to identical twin boys: John Henry Musterman III[1] and Powell Johnson Musterman. The boys were delivered in the upstairs bedroom at home, as most babies were at the time. They were handsome, curly-haired youngsters whom, for some years, Lillian kept immaculately dressed in white. She had no trouble telling them apart if she could just hold them still long enough to place her hand on the head of one or the other. She "felt some difference in the conformation of the skull," and knew immediately which son she was touching. She was never wrong.

When the twins were six years old, a daughter arrived, on May 20, 1916, also born at home. She was named Nancy Elizabeth for her aunts: Nancy Margaret Johnson Parsons and Elizabeth "Lizzie" Musterman Westphal.

After her children were born and the lying-in or confinement[2] was over, Lillian welcomed visits of friends and family, who climbed the stairs, cooed over the new baby, and brought gifts. Nursemaids took care of the children when Lillian returned to work: Edna and Bessie when the boys were babies and Agnes when Nancy was born. Lillian also placed her children on the Cradle Roll at Calvary Methodist Church, where they were christened and attended Sunday school.

Lillian hadn't yet returned to work when, just two weeks after Nancy's birth, her husband suffered a nervous breakdown. That's all the explanation anyone ever gave: nervous breakdown. John remembered his father often sat in the living room on the edge of his chair, elbows on his knees, holding his head with both hands as he rocked back and forth, grimacing in pain. Did he have migraine headaches? Was Nancy's colicky crying unbearable for him? Did an additional child mean an impossible financial situation? It was a "long, incapacitating illness," was the only description given by the family. John was hospitalized at Sheppard-Pratt, a mental hospital in Towson, Maryland, for the next three years.

On Sundays, a Mr. Prosky of West Annapolis drove Lillian to visit her husband. Six days a week, she kept a cheerful manner in the millinery. Each day she pushed Nancy in her buggy to 137 Conduit Street where Aunt Lizzie cared for the baby. Those twin boys probably followed along kicking stones and dragging their satchels of books before they waved goodbye and headed on to Annapolis Elementary School on Green Street. After her long hours in the millinery, Lillian reversed the trip, picking up Nancy and gathering the boys from wherever they were after school. Together they pushed Nancy's carriage back home, stopping at one of the corner greengrocers along the way to buy food for the cook to prepare.

Lillian was exhausted, but she did what she had to do, must do, and actually wanted to do. If she didn't make an income and skimp where she could, she faced losing her children. She was said to be "fierce about keeping her family together."

~

Although their house on Dean Street was considered up-to-date, it wasn't equipped with today's customary appliances. Lillian didn't have a dishwasher to unload or a dryer to empty of clothes when she came home from work. No, she had something better—help. A nurse cared for the babies and a cook prepared dinner. The soiled clothes and linens went to the Chinese laundry at the top of Main Street, or a laundress picked them up and delivered them washed and ironed. Maybe that's how she was able to keep those boys in white.

When she arrived in the evening, Lillian let the nursemaid return to her home and supervised the cook before she set the dining room table. Except for the years he was hospitalized, she chatted with her husband before and after dinner—he in his Morris chair and she in her brocade Queen Anne chair with claw feet, now in a great-granddaughter's home. She rested her tired feet on a little footstool. As the Seth Thomas clock on the mantel struck 8 p.m., Mr. Musterman pointed at it. The children knew it was time to pick up their toys and books and go to bed.

Lillian probably tucked them in and returned to the living room to be warmed by the Latrobe stove that provided the heat to the house. She took up her mending or darned socks by the light of a goose-necked floor lamp embellished with a bit of filigree. Some nights she tightly wrapped strips of pillow ticking or other leftover fabric around rough wooden coat hangers and carefully stitched the cloth. When her daughter grew up, she taught her to do this as well. Their closets were always full of colorful hangers.

According to Lillian's daughter, Nancy:

We had Naval Academy candidates living there [occupying the third-floor rented rooms]. I slept in my parent's bedroom in a crib. We had wardrobes in the rooms for our clothes. Coats were on nails in the back hall.

The rooms also had tiny shallow closets that held only a couple of clothes hangers on a hook mounted flush to the back wall.

One day in 1918, the twins' former nurse came to Lillian to say her husband, John Snowden, was not guilty. He was a Black man wrongly accused of the rape and murder of a white woman.[3] No record exists about how Lillian reacted. The next year, after a trial, the jury found Snowden guilty, a conviction that was formally recognized as a miscarriage of justice in 2001.[4] Mr. Musterman took the twins to the jail on Calvert Street to watch the scaffold being built. Powell remembered watching the tests of the scaffold and trap door.[5]

Family life, visiting her husband, and work demands became more and more difficult for Lillian to manage and she needed some relief. In summer 1919, Lillian placed the boys at Baldwin's farm in Millersville, not far from Annapolis. There they helped pick fruit and perform other farm work. She sent three-year-old Nancy to her Aunt Nan's[6] in Washington, D.C., who by now had four children: Frank, Margaret, Donald, and Douglas. Nancy said:

> Well, we'd all trail up to bed with the oldest leading. One day, as I was standing on the steps on the way up, the front door opened and there were my father and mother. I said, "Have you come to take me home?" I really wanted to go home.

Nancy got her wish. Aunt Nan had secured a French widow for the family to serve as housekeeper, and the family returned to their home on Dean Street. Mr. Musterman also returned as his hospitalization was over, but he never worked again. Lillian continued working for Mrs. Strange. Nancy, who hadn't started school yet, would enjoy sitting in a rocker on the porch with her father in the afternoons. When the *Evening Capital* was delivered, he read the comics to her, including her favorites: "Uncle Wiggly" and "Moon Mullins."

One winter, after a big snow, the twins used a wooden Jell-O crate to form snow blocks for an igloo that the children played in for several days. Nancy helped build a snowman in the front yard. After a big snow, the city blocked the traffic from Dean Street, and the three children rode sleds down the hill in front of their house. During one winter, after a severe ice storm pelted Annapolis, the sidewalks were too slick for Lillian to walk to work. The twins put on their ice skates, brought out their sled, helped their mother sit on it, and skated her to work. It was a ride she talked about for many years.

During the summers when business was slow, Lillian got the family out of the city for a while. One year (probably 1920) she rented a small bungalow in West Annapolis near

Weems Creek. It was situated next to the elementary school and known as "the teacher's house," because single ladies who taught lived there during the school year. Its center hallway went straight through the house from the front door to the back. The doors were left wide open for air circulation. Doorways to the rooms lined the hall on both sides. Agnes, Nancy's nursemaid, bathed the four-year-old in the kitchen in a round galvanized laundry tub. Some days they all went to the creek to paddle in the water and build sand castles along the shore. On one of these occasions, Mr. Musterman, with a twin under each arm, walked into the water up to his chest and let the boys go. That was their first swimming lesson.

Summer also was a time to visit relatives. They rode the train to Baltimore and then another to Ocean City to visit Lillian's sister Abbie. Sometimes they boarded a steamboat in Baltimore and cruised down the Bay to Onancock, Virginia, to visit Lillian's brother George and the children's cousins. The Musterman children swam in the creeks surrounding the town, fed the chickens, chased the ducks around the farmyard, and enjoyed country cooking. When the dinner bell rang, they sat at a table lined with dish after dish of fresh meats from the farm, fish and crab from the creeks, and vegetables from the garden.

During the almost twenty years since Julia Strange had selected the young Lillian Johnson to assist her in her millinery, the two had become close friends. They worked together; took the train to Baltimore together, where they chose the frames, notions, and trims for the millinery; and went on outings together. Julia consoled Lillian when her mother died in 1903, took care of her when she was sick, attended her wedding in 1908, and shared the joy of the twins' birth in 1910. And Lillian stood by Julia when she and her husband divorced in 1912.[7] Lillian probably helped Julia move with her son Robert to her parents' home on Charles Street, just a few blocks from Dean Street. And Julia was a strong support at Nancy's birth and Mr. Musterman's hospitalization. All those years, the two women continued to work together at the hat shop at 205 Main Street.[8]

In September 1918, a small ad appeared in the newspaper when they needed a "young lady in millinery" as well as an errand girl.[9] In October Mrs. Strange's new hats were described in a front page story "Stylish Display of Fall Millinery."[10] About this time the Spanish flu was sweeping Annapolis and it was a "stricken city ... one passed daily a heap of new coffins piled on the sidewalk and in the street [East Street] itself."[11] Front page stories in the *Evening Capital* listed who was sick and who had died as the epidemic raged. Lillian must have been afraid for her children when she read about the illness striking her neighbors just a few doors down from the Musterman home on Dean Street.[12]

Just as the flu ravaged Annapolis, Julia Strange left the millinery. Perhaps she was also a victim. She was in her early-to-mid-forties. Lillian, now thirty-seven, and Miriam Pettit Tilghman, wife of the future well-known jeweler,[13] took over the business briefly. It appears that Lillian kept the business going on her own.[14] Lillian said, "I stayed with her [Julia Strange] until her death and then I worked with her sister."[15]

"What do I do now?" Lillian must have cried out when she learned of Mrs. Strange's death. She was certainly at her wits' end. Although she had been on her own when she went to Baltimore as a young woman, this was different. Now she had three children. Now she had an incapacitated husband. Now, as before, she had little money.

Yet she was a well-known and established milliner with her own clientele. She would come up with something. And she knew—probably always knew—what she was to do next.

Work in a hat shop, but not anyone else's. It had to be *her* hat shop. A business known as L.P. Musterman's. And it must be on Main Street.

But how to do it? That was her challenge.

7

A Shop of Her Own

LILLIAN BROUGHT HER HUSBAND home from the hospital in the fall of 1919 and her children home as well—Nancy from her Aunt Nan's and the boys from Baldwin's farm. Mr. Musterman was now a very silent man who sat and read. The French housekeeper, whom Lillian's sister Nan had hired for them, ran the house. Lillian had no time to even think about the hot political topic of the day—women getting the vote. She had enough to do keeping her family together and her business viable. After Julia Strange's death, Lillian was thinking, wondering, and planning how to get her own shop. She remembered:

> It was a year before I found the shop and more [time] to buy it. I went to [its owner] George Feldmeyer, a very good friend of the family, and said: "I want that building. I know it's up for sale, but I can't think of buying that building. Promise me that you'll let me have the [right of] refusal of it, if anybody comes [to buy it]. I can't ask you to hold it for me, but I'm asking for the refusal of it." So he said, "I don't know

if I have anyone … ." I never thought to ask him if anybody really wanted it or not. He was a friend of my husband's. So for the next two years I rented it.[1]

The building Lillian wanted was 197 Main Street.

Dr. Feldmeyer had bought the house in 1897, when it still had its Revolutionary-Era appearance. He completely renovated it into a grand Victorian-style home,[2] and by 1900 his family was living there. From there it was just a few short steps to his dental office up Main Street.[3]

But by 1920, the Feldmeyers had moved to yet another new home at 2 Southgate Avenue, in "the suburbs." The house at 197 Main Street stood empty, just when Lillian needed it.

During the two years she rented the house, Lillian may have sublet the rooms she wasn't using for her millinery. She certainly used the parlors, welcoming customers to the front one. From the sidewalk, the ladies were barely able to see her sample hats through the big bay window. They craned their necks to get a better look. They climbed the six steps to rap on the outer door, where she welcomed them in and ushered them through the vestibule, asking how they were. She likely led them by a table display of hats and notions. Certainly they settled into one of the chairs near the window, where the light streamed in and they could catch a glimpse of the State House dome through the alley across the street. On the table would be copies of *The Milliner* to page through and see the latest styles. A large mirror hung nearby on the wall for customers to admire themselves.

Lillian's daughter Nancy remembered that her mother rented the building for two years for her business, and then:

> She took every penny she had and bought that house at 197 Main Street. The date was June 2, 1921. Dr. George Feldmeyer loaned her the money. She was years paying off that mortgage—she must have had that mortgage for 50 years. Dr. George kept extending it [the loan] so that she could keep the store.

Once she had her mortgage,[4] Ruby Westphal Chaney, Lillian's close friend and her husband's niece, helped her borrow more money from a local bank. With these funds, it was Lillian's turn to change 197 Main Street to suit herself. She set about remodeling to create the perfect shop just as she had once retrimmed a buckram base to create the perfect Gainsborough hat.

She started at the entrance to the house by removing the stairs and vestibule's outer door, breaking through the brick wall, and installing new stairs from the sidewalk to the interior double wooden door, just as it remains today. Inside, she left the hallways, staircases, dining room, and kitchen on the first floor, and the second- and third-floor rooms, as they were. She pulled shut the heavy pocket doors separating the dining room from the two parlors, walling off any possible entry from the house to her store.

Her store space took up the area of the two first-floor parlors. After removing the old parlor floors, she installed a new floor at street level. She also removed the overhanging bay window, broke through the stone foundation, and extended the store about three feet onto the sidewalk.

Next came her new storefront. Rather than tiny panes as most stores on Main Street featured, she installed one large plate-glass picture window. It was mounted on a solid cement base that enclosed a wide wooden sill—also about three feet deep—framed by two tall glass panels on the left and right sides.

With her shop entrance now level with the sidewalk, passersby could see her hats on display on the sill as well as those inside as they walked up and down Main Street. No longer would customers struggle to look through the high bay window or need to climb stairs to the shop's front door. From street level, they could open a new wood-framed glass door sheltered from the elements and hear a tiny brass bell tinkle as they entered.[5]

After the window was in place, up went brown paper to hide the interior. No one on the street could see what was going on inside. In the shop space, shelves were installed on the back and side walls, almost to the ceiling. A deep counter with wide drawers ran the width of the showroom to separate the selling area from the wrapping area and cash drawer. Her workroom was one step up behind the counter and included a small lavatory. She placed her two treadle sewing machines— an electric sewing machine joined them some years later— below shelves stocked with sewing threads of all colors, veils, ribbons, and artificial flowers. A steam kettle, ironing board, and hat blocks found a home. A small window at the back let in a bit of light from the yard and alley.

When the glass cases and hat stands arrived, she supervised their careful placement on one side of the shop floor.

On the left wall toward the front and visible from the street she hung a magnificent diamond-dust mirror. It stretched to the ceiling. There the gilt Rococo filigree arched over a marble shelf at the base, on which rested a hand mirror. A velvet bench was ready for the forty-five years of ladies who would sit and preen as they admired both the front and back of the hats they were considering.

As the renovation neared completion, Lillian began ordering supplies from the finest millineries. The days of true millinery and custom-designed hats were waning by the 1920s, so she needed both hat bases and finished hats—wide brim and cloche, straw and felt, some with trimmings, some without—to fill her store.

By September, boxes started arriving. Hats appeared everywhere. On the shelves that lined the walls and filling the two glass cabinets. Atop the tall brass floor stands. On the short brass stands on the counters. Even in a nook above the wainscoting that cleverly hid a fireplace. She filled the wide storefront display shelf with hats. The drawers, too, held hats, ready for replenishing when the visible stock was sold. Laces and feathers and flowers and spools of velvet and grosgrain ribbon—all she needed to trim a hat, old or new, however the wearer wanted—were arranged to add a touch of color to the displays. More than one hundred hats were available at L.P. Musterman's. Straight from New York and Baltimore. The latest styles. Every size. And they could be stretched, lined, re-trimmed, and steamed by the well-known Annapolis milliner, Mrs. Musterman.

Announcements went out. Advertisements appeared. The brown paper came down. Lillian was ready. The opening was the talk of the town. Let the customers come!

8

The Key to Her Success

S HE HAD DONE IT—LILLIAN had her hat shop.

    She attained her goal, and the inevitable followed: more hard work and effort to act on that achievement. A goal is not an end but a beginning. At the same time, life continues making demands and forcing decisions. It brings joys and sorrows. So it was for Lillian.

She had her customers. She also had her growing children, a disabled husband, a household to run, bills to pay, church to attend, and community activities to support. Most important for survival was keeping her hat shop successful for years to come.

Running the business, though demanding, was probably the most exciting, most pleasurable part of Lillian's day. Since her short apprenticeship in Baltimore and arrival in Annapolis, she had been in the millinery business for more than twenty years on the day of her store's 1921 grand opening. Millinery had become a different business. Gone were the days when she created a unique hat by first forming an iron frame and next adding fabric, feathers, and flowers. Now ready-made hats filled the windows of both the hat shops and general merchandise stores in every town in the country. Lillian adjusted to those changes and sold ready-made hats. But that didn't mean her skills went to waste or were forgotten.

When a customer sat at the gilt Rococo mirror, Lillian stood behind and suggested "maybe a flower here" or "perhaps a feather just there" as she held a bright item to perk up a rather dull straw hat or add flair to a felt cloche. Sometimes she held a bit of veiling to soften the look. When the customer was pleased, Lillian pinned the additional trim and a slip of paper with the customer's name to the hat, and took it to her workroom. Later that day when the shop was quiet, she threaded a needle and tacked the embellishment to the hat. Sometimes she steamed a brim to curve it differently for the face it was to frame. When a hat was a bit tight, she put it on a wooden hat stretcher and cranked it out a couple of turns. There it stayed for a few days to increase its size. Once the hat was just what the customer wanted, Lillian wrapped it in tissue and placed it in one of her six-sided maroon boxes with "L.P. Musterman Hat Shop" printed on the pink lid. Ready for pick up or delivery.

During the Depression years, Lillian's original skills became even more important as penny-pinching women and those making do through the lean times brought their last season's hat to her for remodeling and retrimming. Her skills were needed right up until she retired in the mid-1960s.

She remembered a customer telling her: "I never look in the mirror. All I do is see Mrs. Musterman. If she shakes her head, I know it isn't mine."[1] Another customer—Betsy Davis—bought several hats from L.P. Musterman's over the years. When she married, she did not want a wedding dress and veil for the ceremony. Instead, she remembered: "I told Mrs. Musterman I wanted a hat with a small veil in front and coming just above the shoulders in the back. She fixed me up with exactly what I wanted!!! She was so very sweet!!!"

When Shirley Wilsman (now Kimi Kim-Ng) was in her late teens and early twenties, she "bought many hats from Mrs. Musterman and just loved that store. … one of my favorite hats back in the early 1960s … was a big red wide-brimmed straw." Another favorite was a Navy blue straw which she loaned to her little sister to go with a blue seersucker outfit to wear to their other sister's wedding. Shirley herself wore the red. "The wedding reception was at the Naval Academy Alumni House. It was a real faux pas." Certainly if Lillian had known she would have told the young lady what she herself realized later: "It [my hat] garnered so much attention and took the focus off my sister. But I was so young and naïve at the time I didn't realize that was a no-no!"[2]

Lillian's regular customers included her many nieces and cousins; fellow members of her Calvary Methodist Church woman's circle, Zonta Club, and Eastern Star; and other Annapolis ladies and girls. The faculty wives of St. John's College and the Naval Academy came to her store. Newly arrived Navy wives quickly learned where to buy the latest hats—at Mrs. Musterman's. They wore the very best during the years their husbands were stationed at the Naval Academy.

"The Navy folks had to have lots of hats," she said. "Most women owned about three or four. Some women were more like friends than customers and we'd visit when they came." They stopped by the store each spring and fall to buy a hat of the latest style or pick up a bargain at the end-of-season sale.

Lillian remembered a woman who was tired from a day of shopping on Main Street and was on her way home. "May I come in and rest for a while?" she asked.

"Of course."

"I'm not going to buy, I'm not buying."

"Now I didn't ask you to buy, did I?"

"No."

Lillian remembered: "She came in and sat down. We started talking and I never mentioned a hat. Then she said, 'Do you have any new hats?' I sat her down in front of the mirror. Well! I know I sold her $50 worth of hats before she left—more than three. They were about $10 then."

Her clientele also included the city's women of color. At that time, before the end of segregation, these customers usually were not invited to try on hats themselves. Instead, one of Lillian's assistants, or occasionally one of her grand-daughters, modeled various hats the lady selected until she decided which she preferred. Occasionally Lillian asked the customer to place a piece of paper on her head in order to try the hat herself. But the late "Miss Peggy"—Ethelda "Peggy" Kimbo—the hostess and later a waitress at Little Campus Inn (now Galway Bay Irish Pub and Restaurant) remembered that "not all Colored people were allowed to try on hats, but Mrs. Musterman let my mother. She was so dear."[3]

For over thirty years, one woman traveled from New York—spring and fall— to complete her new outfit for the season with a hat from L.P. Musterman's. From the 1920s through the 1940s, Mrs. Sima, wife of the Naval Academy bandmaster, was a regular customer. She played the piano at the Republic Theatre movie house for the silent, black-and-white films just a few doors down from the shop—always in a lovely hat. Other special customers were the mother of Governor Albert C. Ritchie in the 1920s and 1930s, and the wife of Governor J. Millard Tawes in the 1950s and 1960s.

In the 1920s, Lillian's twin sons delivered hats on their second-hand bike for twenty-five cents a week plus tips. They vied for deliveries to Mrs. Sima, saying, "She was always good for a dime tip."[4] Neighborhood children also delivered her hats over the years. In the 1920s and 1930s, the Bounelis girls—Helen, Catherine, and Donna—who lived across the street above their parents' business, the Capital Restaurant, got five cents for every hat they delivered.[5] At Lillian's funeral years later, a priest who just happened to be in Annapolis at the time said he read about her death and viewing. He couldn't miss the opportunity to honor her memory, be with the family, and share his memories of delivering hats for Mrs. Musterman in the 1940s. In the 1950s, her paper boy, Roscoe C. Rowe, III, ran hats to his grandmother to try. He returned with either money "to pay Mrs. Musterman for the hat" or the hat.[6]

"Twice a year," Lillian said, "I went to New York for the new styles, and I always took my assistant. In between those times, I'd get on a bus on Sunday afternoon, buy on Monday morning and come back." She also ordered some of her hats and notions from salesmen who stopped by the shop throughout the year.

Her friend Ruby Chaney often traveled with her on the buying trips to New York, and sometimes her daughter enjoyed the trip too. At various millinery houses, they viewed the latest models and chose the best. They also selected trimming supplies: veils, flowers, feathers, berries, and ribbons. At the end of a long day, they were wined and dined by the salesmen before enjoying a Broadway show. The Baltimore millinery wholesalers, such as Armstrong, Cator & Co., were close enough for a day trip of selecting and buying hats and notions in the city. One of the Baltimore salesmen, Eric Lowenthal, often took Lillian to Miller Brothers for lunch. "She especially enjoyed the lobster," he said.[7]

～

Lillian never missed a chance to get a notice for L.P. Musterman's in the *Evening Capital*. She advertised the season openings and sales. Hers was one of the many business cards that appeared on full-page "season's greeting" displays at Thanksgiving, Christmas, Easter, and Mother's Day.

But her hat store was not the only one advertising. In fact, Mrs. M.F. Holidayoke's millinery advertisements appeared in the paper as early as 1887; L.H. Rehn's ad for "Spring Hats of Straw and Silk" appeared on the same page.[8] While Lillian and Julia Strange were working together in September 1912, the new season of hats available at Holidayoke's made front page news—and that story appeared higher on the page than news about Prince Axel of Denmark's visit to the Naval Academy.[9] A few days later, a "Miss L. M. Woolley" also got a paragraph announcing "new winter hats may be viewed on Tuesdays and Wednesdays" at her three millinery parlors at the Arundel Building, Church Circle, and West Street.[10] A front-page story on October 1, 1918, described Julia Strange's fall opening as showing "many exquisite designs … a brown velvet with wild roses embroidered on the brim … with simplicity and elegance …."[11]

In the 1930s (and perhaps earlier) the Dollar Hat Shop was a competitor located at the foot of Main Street at 129, next to Snyder Bros. Bakery at 131.[12] But it was Holidayoke's ads that somehow always managed to get a notice in the paper right under Lillian's when both stores advertised their spring or fall openings well into the 1950s.

Anticipation for the new season's hats was always high. Women scanned the paper for an ad stating: "Mrs. Musterman and Mrs. Kashner have returned from New York with Spring Hats" in February or "with new velvets" in the fall. Sometimes a simple advertisement appeared in the *Evening Capital* for a couple of weeks in a plain lined box stating the date and time for the opening at L.P. Musterman's Hat Shop. Sometimes she paid extra for a line: "Hats Make the Difference." Invitations were sent to regular customers. Some *very* special customers were invited for a sneak preview. Others saw samples of the new models at one of the fashion shows sponsored by the charities a week or two before.

The day before the grand opening, her hat shop was closed to business. The window was papered over. The out-of-season hats were put away. The shop was polished, decorated, and refurbished. Fresh flowers were placed among the ferns, elephant ears, spider plants, and her famous African violets that blossomed with colors rivaling the many hues of her hats. (Somehow those African violets were always in bloom.) The new hats were arranged to their best advantage. When the door was unlocked on opening day, a throng of expectant ladies quickly filled the shop oohing and aahing their way around the new merchandise.

Hats sold quickly at the beginning of each season, then sales slowed to a trickle. Soon appeared the advertisement "Great Reduction in Summer Hats" to announce the end-of-the-season sale in July; a similar one in February featured a clearance of fall hats. Customers trying on sale hats often saw large cardboard boxes being opened, paper strewn every-where, and new hats being held up as Lillian briefly admired them and decided the price. As soon as she stated the amount, her assistant wrote it on a tag, looped the tag through the hat label, and tucked the hat in one of the big drawers.

"What's that? Let me see . . ." a curious customer said, heading toward the commotion near the workroom. "Never you mind, you'll see it at my opening next week," Lillian said as she ushered the woman back to the sale hats.

In addition to her advertisements, Lillian's activities often appeared in the *Evening Capital*. In October 1929, a story told of the local chapter of the Catholic Daughters of America's raffling a doll that could be seen in the hat shop display win-dow. Large groups of children gathered at "most hours of the day" to view the beautiful, child-size doll dressed in "sports frock, knitted hat and white shoes and stockings. She [the doll] has ignored the vogue for bobbed hair and has gleaming golden curls falling around her shoulders."[13]

Luncheons and fashion shows often featured Lillian's hats. At one event, a group of military wives arrived at a luncheon at the Officer's Club to find an array of doilies, blossoms, bal-loons, ribbons, and other materials on the tables. Their task— make a hat. The women who created the winning hats—most attractive and funniest—were awarded a hat from L.P. Musterman Hat Shop.[14]

~

Through the years, Lillian trained several excellent assistants. She hired Flora Kashner when she was a young woman. Mrs. K, as many called her, worked in the store until the end of her life in the 1950s. Another wonderful sales lady was Mrs. Pearl Zang, Lillian's last assistant in the hat shop. Mrs. Zang was widely read and had a great memory for names—a big help as the years went by. Her engaging conversation entertained customers as they tried on hats, and maybe kept them in the store just long enough to buy. When Lillian opened the hat shop in 1921, Eva Owings worked with her, followed by Edith Jones and a Mrs. Moore. During the busy season, part-time assistants were hired as well. They all had long tenures and worked long hours, especially in the 1920s when the shop was open until 9 p.m. every day.

Lillian also hired teenagers and trained them as well as she had trained Mrs. Kashner and Mrs. Zang. Anne Hagen (now Pidkowicz), a high school senior in the late 1940s, walked from St. Mary's to the hat shop after school each day and drove the twenty-five miles from her home in Owensville on Saturdays. "Mrs. Musterman was quite the taskmaster," Anne said. But she didn't mind. So was her mother. "Be polite, do your work fast and well, learn what the customer wants, and never argue with a customer." Anne learned a lot about sales that year. And much about hats. How to steam them, stretch them, tilt them, add a veil. Recently she reminisced: "Mrs. Musterman was so gracious. Everyone loved her. And she trusted me to get to the shop early on Saturdays and open by myself."

That year, the fall and winter season's hats were selling well. But try as they might, no one in the store could sell one particular, expensive hat. "We all thought it was the ugliest in the shop." Even with their combined sales prowess, "Mrs. Kashner and Mrs. Musterman could not get rid of it. It was a brown fall felt with weird feathers on it. Of course, we didn't call it 'ugly' in front of Mrs. Musterman." One day Anne was waiting on a difficult older lady who tried on every hat in the store.

> Nothing suited her! She let me know she was hard to please, and said our inventory did not measure up to her standards! That made me angry. Everyone in town knew Mrs. Musterman had the very latest styles and the most beautiful hats. I decided to show this customer the Ugly hat. I told her the hat was the finest, most expensive hat in the shop! It was obvious to me that that was her measure of a good hat. She bought it. Mrs. Musterman was pleased. That was all I needed.[15]

Yes, Lillian was an entrepreneur par excellence. Well known for her beautiful hats, welcoming personality, and excellent assistants. She succeeded with an approach that, like her store, she never changed during the more than forty years she was in business. Spring and fall. Year after year. Buying trips to New York and Baltimore. End-of-season sales. Brown-paper-covered windows. Great anticipation among the ladies of Annapolis. The advertising. The opening. The rush to try on this, consider that. The perfect hat to match a dress for tea or a coat for travel. Many a lady stepped out the door to the sidewalk on Main Street proudly holding an L.P. Musterman hat box. As Sharie Valereo said about the store, "Yes, it was one of a kind!"[16]

~

Today it would be impossible for a woman, even one as talented as Lillian, to support a family as a milliner, selling only hats. But until the mid-1960s, a hat was a necessity. Since ancient Egypt, people have worn hats. In the seventeenth century, a lady's hat was a sign of wealth, but by the nineteenth century, women of all classes wore hats.[17] It was unthinkable for a woman to leave her home without a hat. It was the essential accessory. And not just for church or temple services. No woman arrived uncovered to a tea, a luncheon, a wedding, or a funeral. No women dared even to step onto the train platform to catch the B&A to Baltimore to shop without wearing a hat. Emily Post admonished in 1959: "It is impossible for a woman to appear chic without a hat."[18] And not only women. Everyone, whether rich or poor, young or old, man or woman, boy or girl, wore a hat whenever they went out the door.

Lillian donned her own hat each morning for her walk from Dean Street to her store, and again each evening for her return. And even after the family moved to Main Street to live above the store, she rarely went out the door uncovered. Every morning she descended the stairway inside her home, selected a hat from the rack in the hall, secured it on her head with a hat pin, exited to the sidewalk, walked by her hat display in the shop's window to the store entrance, and unlocked the door. Once inside, she placed her hat on a peg in the workroom where it remained until she stepped out again. Musterman's was open for another day of business.

9

LIFE ABOVE THE STORE

*L*ILLIAN RECOGNIZED THAT THE Musterman family's survival depended on her business success, and fortunately the business itself was her love. She arrived early each morning to unlock the store, was ready for customers by 8 a.m.—in later years by 9 a.m.—and locked the door at 5 p.m., 9:30 p.m. on Saturdays. Then she walked the five blocks to her home on Dean Street. There awaiting her were the growing children, her husband, and the household chores.

And the bills.

Lillian carried the burden of the family finances. Her husband's medical bills. Groceries. Children's shoes and coats. The household supplies. Her maid and laundress. The rent for the Dean Street home. The loan repayments to Dr. Feldmeyer for the large building with her store. She calculated the income from her sales and the rented areas above the store on Main Street. Surely she pondered how to make ends meet as she walked to and from the hat shop each day.

In winter she faced bitter winds and icy sidewalks. Summer brought sweltering heat and humidity. On rainy days she arrived soaking wet and dripped her way across the shop floor to her workroom.

On one of those walks, the solution came to her: Give up the house and live above the store. The twin boys—John and Powell—were now twelve years old. Nancy was six and ready to start first grade in the fall. The boys could walk with her to the elementary school on Green Street just down the hill. With Mr. Musterman right upstairs, Lillian could check on him at lunch time and he could watch Nancy after school.

It was decided. They would move.

Lillian borrowed yet more money to redecorate the new living quarters for her family. Rooms were painted. Walls were papered. Two large porches were added to the back of the house on both the first and second floors. Both spanned the width of the house and were about sixteen feet deep. Effectively creating another living space, the porches were the only place to catch a summer breeze in this city home, the second-floor porch particularly. It looked out over the side alley leading up to Ridout Alley on one side, the houses of Duke of Gloucester Street at the back, and the Moss family home's second-floor windows and rooftop on the other side at 195 Main Street. A bit of sun peeked in to warm Lillian's flower boxes. A night-blooming jasmine scented the evening air. Here in summer after a hot day waiting on customers in her store, Lillian rested in a metal rocking chair, untied and took off her shoes, and put her tired feet up on a footstool.

Once the house was ready, the Mustermans moved in and took over the first and second floors. The children could run up and down the stairs until scolded, sneak up the hidden staircase, play on the porches, or dig in the sunless dirt yard where nothing ever grew. The cook prepared meals in the kitchen and the family gathered to eat in the dining room on the first floor. On the second floor, in addition to four bedrooms and a large bathroom, Mr. Musterman read in the front room that was directly over the store. This sun-filled room was the family sitting room. It faced Main Street and had a view of the Maryland State Capital dome. By leaning out of the windows, the children could look up the street and see St. Anne's Episcopal Church or down the street to the city dock. They had front-row seats for parades or just people-watching—shoppers on Saturday, church-goers on Sunday. By living on Main Street, the Mustermans were, as Ralph Crosby stated in his book *Memoirs of a Main Street Boy*, "at the epicenter of small town life."[1]

Nancy, who no longer had friends right next door as she did on Dean Street, would spread out her dolls on the sitting room floor after school and play alone until dinner time. The Seth Thomas clock on the mirrored mantel tick-tocked and chimed as she talked to them. Nearby her father sat quietly reading in his big, green-leather Morris chair. As Nancy dressed her dolls, moved them around, and created pretend conversations, Mr. Musterman asked her about them and what they were doing.

A huge black-and-white-tiled bathroom on the second floor had doors to the hall, the front bedroom, and the back bedroom. None of the doors ever shut tightly. In the back corner next to a marble sink was the commode on a cement pedestal. When anyone sat on the throne, they listened for the sound of approaching footsteps and darted their eyes from one door to the other, ready to holler if a glass doorknob turned or a door started to creak open. Some days, Mr. Musterman helped Nancy to wash her hair as she stood on the hamper and leaned over the sink. Because her mother worked, her father did "everything a mother would do," she later said.

Lillian let Nancy give up her crib when they moved to Main Street and they both slept in the front bedroom. The boys and Mr. Musterman had the back rooms. Most of the rooms had radiators in front of closed fireplaces. The back stairway, once used by maids to run from floor to floor when the Feldmeyers lived there, became closets and storage areas. A gas light receptacle remained in one of the back stairways— not removed when the house was "electrified" with outlets, ceiling lights, and push-button switches in all the rooms.

Lillian also created a one-bedroom apartment with sitting room and kitchen on the third floor. It was rented for all the years she lived on Main Street. The first tenant was a "Nurse Nyce," who had cared for old Mrs. Feldmeyer. Many tenants followed, including Reida Longanecker and Katherine M. Kibler, both school teachers who became good friends.[2] And that was important because Lillian had not created a private entrance to the apartment. Tenants used the same street entrance and stairs as the family to get to the second floor. Tenants continued down the second-floor hall that the family used to get from room to room to reach the staircase that led to the third floor and their apartment. Whoever entered the house, as well as their sounds, traveled up the steep stairs and along the halls. The setup required a lot of trust and respect for one another's privacy in this less than private arrangement.

The boys adjusted well to living on Main Street. Life in town meant they could roam the city and join their friends for a soda at the drug store or take in a movie just a few doors down at the Republic Theater. But throughout that first year on Main Street, Lillian often came home to an unhappy daughter. Nancy wasn't allowed to walk around town on her own and missed her friends. When she started first grade, she hated it. Her teacher Mrs. Hoffman was strict and often put Nancy in the corner or denied her recess for minor infractions at best or excusable actions at worst. One day Nancy helped her friend Carrie Jefferson from Dean Street get her stuck finger out of the curlicue ironwork of her desk. Both girls were severely scolded. Lillian listened to a tearful Nancy plead: "Please don't send me to school, I'm just going to die if I have to go." Sometimes Lillian did allow Nancy to miss a day. That first year was terrible for Nancy, but after that she loved her teachers. Occasionally if she did come into the shop after school with tears in her eyes, Lillian would say "Let's go down to Read's [drugstore] and get a Coke. We'll talk about it."

On weekends Mr. Musterman took Nancy on long walks. Sometimes to visit his sister's or brother's families, sometimes across the Spa Creek bridge to Eastport or over the Severn River Bridge to Pendennis Mount. On June 14, 1924, they sat together on the hillside overlooking the new Severn River Bridge and viewed the opening ceremonies. This masonry drawbridge replaced the first road bridge to cross the Severn River—a wooden drawbridge built in 1886.[3]

Lillian made most of Nancy's clothes, her doll's clothes, and her costumes until she was a teenager. She made Nancy a veil and train when she had the starring role as the bride of Tom Thumb—in the annual production at Calvary Methodist Church. John had played Tom Thumb in 1915.[4] The night before Nancy's performance, Lillian tied her daughter's hair in rags so the next day she had curls instead of her straight Dutch bob. Lillian also made a costume of green cambric trimmed in silver tinsel for Nancy's dance recital at the Circle Theater. One Easter, she made Nancy an A-line dress of pink taffeta decorated with a blue bow. Its long streamers reached to the hem. While she never had many clothes, Nancy found plenty of trim in the store to change the look of her outfits. Lillian taught her daughter to sew as she grew older, but Nancy said her mother often ripped out any work not up to her standards.

Lillian also did some cooking. She made fruit cake each Christmas, cookies, and crab apple jelly. Scrapple, fried bacon rind, and crab cakes. She soaked chicken pieces in milk overnight for frying the next day. Her apple sauce was unique. After she boiled the apples, she put them through a ricer to separate the pulp from the skin, core, and seeds. While the apple sauce was still hot, she stirred in some "Red Hots," those tiny little tart candies, to add cinnamon flavor and color. She skinned mushrooms before cooking and also skinned peaches under water—something about the feel of the fuzzy skin repelled her. When they were available, she served Chincoteague oysters—one of her favorite foods from the Eastern Shore of her youth.

Evening events, such as her church circle meetings, were sometimes held in her home. She often went with Mr. Musterman to the movies or to the Masonic Lodge for Knights Templar events. In 1921, the year she was busy remodeling and opening her new store, she managed to find the time to help found the new Eastern Star chapter. Together with her close friend Ruby Chaney, forty-eight other women, and twenty-five men, she became a charter member of Tuscana Chapter #24 on February 8, 1921. Initiation fees were $5. Eleven months later membership was up to 160 persons. After it was formed, the Mustermans often went to Eastern Star events.

While their parents were out, John and Powell babysat for Nancy. One night one twin said, "Go to the back bedroom, Nancy." So she did. The room was dark and quiet. All of a sudden the other twin jumped out of the wardrobe, draped in a sheet, arms outstretched. "Boo!" Poor Nancy was scared to death. Some nights they got under her bed and bounced it up and down. They told her ghost stories and did "other funny little tricks." But those playful boys were also good to her. The twins were always tinkering. They made phones, radios, and teletypes. They fixed the wiring on lamps and appliances. And they taught Nancy how to fix lights and switches and other things around the house. She learned so much from her brothers that she aced her physics exams when she got to high school.

Just before Christmas, December 23, 1924, Lillian went down the street to the market to buy a Christmas tree and returned home to await delivery. She climbed the stairs to fix lunch. There on the living room floor she found her husband. Dead.

She sent a message to the schools for Nancy to come home from third grade and the boys from high school. Nancy remembered being excited at the thought her mother planned to take her to Baltimore for some last-minute Christmas shopping. But when the children arrived home, their mother sat them down and said, "Your daddy has died, and you are not to cry." Next she got out their Christmas presents. Among them was a cradle for Nancy's favorite doll, Mary. Her father had made it from a peach basket. He had carved wooden rockers and attached an old clock spring to support the canopy. Lillian had covered it in pink with net and made the mattress, pillow, and linens for it.

Over Christmas and the days following, the casket sat on a bier in the living room, open and surrounded by funeral sprays. Throughout her life, the smell of carnations always haunted Nancy. "After Christmas, on the day of the funeral, someone picked me up to kiss him goodbye before they closed the casket," she remembered. But Lillian didn't let Nancy attend the funeral because she believed her daughter was too young and too sad. Instead Nancy walked up Main Street to stay with her much older cousins, Andrew and Bertha Musterman, in their apartment in the Maryland Inn.

Mr. Musterman was sixty-five years old when he suffered his fatal heart attack. Lillian was forty-three. When she contemplated the years of widowhood that lay ahead, she wondered what else could possibly befall her.

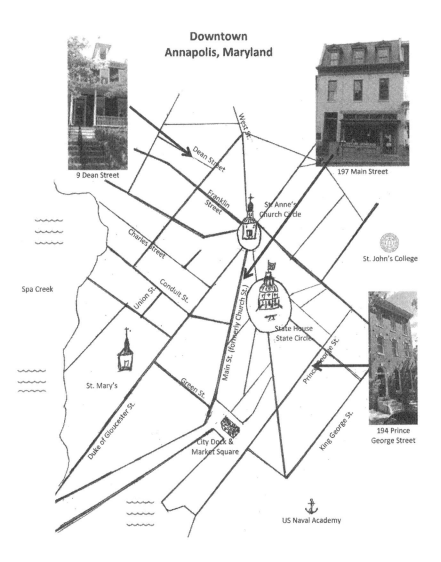

Downtown Annapolis, Maryland

9 Dean Street

197 Main Street

West St.

Dean Street

Franklin Street

St. Anne's Church Circle

Charles Street

St. John's College

Spa Creek

Conduit St.

Union St.

Main St. (formerly Church St.)

State House State Circle

Prince George St.

St. Mary's

Green St.

King George St.

194 Prince George Street

Duke of Gloucester St.

City Dock & Market Square

US Naval Academy

Lillian was about twenty when she arrived in Annapolis, Maryland, and lived there until her last breath at ninety-eight. First in the Feldmeyer-Gassaway House on Prince George Street, where she met John Musterman; the next ten years on Dean Street; and above her hat shop on Main Street from 1922 until she moved to a nursing home in Eastport in the 1970s.

Margaret "Peggie" Anne Johnson née FitzGerald
(1842–1902)

Lillian grew up in Onancock, Virginia, at 10 Holly Street (no longer standing) with her mother and four siblings.

Thomas Johnson (Cap'n Tom)
(1809–1906)

Lillian's home was next to her
grandfather Johnson's farm house.

Margaret Anne Jane FitzGerald
née Hopkins (1822–1903)

Lillian visited her "Grandma FitzGerald" in her home at 26 King
Street. It is a "big house, little house, colonnade, and kitchen" style,
typical of the Eastern Shore.

Lillian and her friend Miss Rowe in their
Gainsborough hats, which were all the rage
at the turn of the century.
(c 1900)

Lillian apprenticed at Armstrong Cators
in Baltimore and filled assignments in
Western Maryland where she met many other milliners.
(c 1900)

Lillian Powell Johnson
(1881–1980)
Lillian was hired on the spot when Julia Strange,
an Annapolis milliner, learned
Lillian could "sew velvet to buckram."

John Henry Musterman
(1859–1924)

John was quite the dandy in his high silk hat and
the most eligible bachelor in Annapolis,
but his bachelor days were numbered when
Lillian came to town.

The Widow and Children of the First John Henry Musterman of
Annapolis: Anna Catharina, Louis Henry (in chair),
John Henry, Catherine Elizabeth, Andrew Hermann
(c 1870)

John Henry Musterman was the oldest child of
his German immigrant father of the same name.
John's mother, also an immigrant, was Anna Catharina Rehn.

John Henry Musterman
(c 1880s)

John Musterman signing dance cards amid a bevy of young ladies.
John was a Mason, a partner in a pharmacy, and clerk at the
Naval Academy.

Lillian lodged with the Feldmeyer sisters on
Prince George Street where she met John Musterman.
Pictured are Lillian Johnson, George Feldmeyer, John Musterman in
top hat, and the Fedmeyer sisters (young man unknown).
(c 1900)

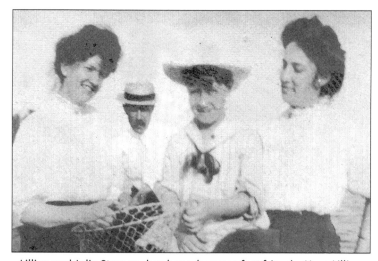

Lillian and Julia Strange, her boss, became fast friends. Here Lillian
and John Musterman are crabbing with Julia and her son Robert.
(c 1908)

John and Lillian got to know each other on
day's outings around town.
(c 1905)

Abbie Hayman, Lillian's sister, spent the summers in Ocean City.
Lillian and John visited her and her family there often.
(c 1905)

The boys were cared for by several nurses. Here one
has a twin under each arm.
(1910)

John Musterman with his twin sons, John and Powell,
on the lawn in front of their home at 9 Dean Street.
(1911)

Lillian holding her new baby daughter Nancy Elizabeth.
Lillian always dressed the boys in white.
(1916)

Lillian made most of Nancy's clothes and costumes.
Here Nancy is dressed as Tom Thumb's Bride
for the annual pageant at
Calvary Methodist Church.
(1921)

Powell, Nancy, and John Musterman
(c 1920)

Lillian remodeled the ground floor of the house at 197 Main Street
and opened L.P. Musterman Hat Shop in 1921.
It was the talk of the town.

When the hat shop reopened in September
after the April 1957 fire, little had changed
from her original except the addition
of air conditioning.

The diamond-dust Rococo mirror seen through the
shop window drew in passersby to the hat shop.

Lillian adjusts a hat for a customer seated at the gilt mirror.
(Model, Mrs. C. Rucker; photographer, R. W. Linfield.)
(*Annapolis Faces,* c 1963)

Lillian received so many bouquets on her reopening after
the fire that she wondered was she selling hats or flowers?
(1957)

Lillian's workroom was up a couple of steps
at the back of the store.

The buildings at 195 and 197 Main Street were once
a coffee shop, later a candy store and hat shop,
and now a sushi café.
(2019)

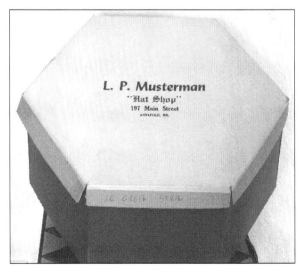

Hats were carefully wrapped in tissue and placed in an
L.P. Musterman Hat Shop box for her customers.

Twice a year Lillian traveled to New York
to buy the next season's hats. She often went
with Ruby Chaney and her daughter Nancy.
(c 1930)

Powell, Nancy, John, and Lillian Musterman
(c 1930)

John, Lillian, and Powell Musterman
(c 1937)

Lillian Powell Musterman
(c 1930)

Nancy and Her Finacée, Midshipman Tom Reed
(1935)

Nancy Musterman Reed dressed all in green
from head to toe for her wedding. It was the
perfect traveling suit with its soutache jacket
for the couple's New York honeymoon.
(September 1936)

Lillian's growing family: John (or Powell), Peg, Lou, Lillian, Nancy M.
Reed, Powell (or John), Tom Reed, Peggy and Nancy.
(Easter day, April 9, 1939)

Lillian's family enjoys swimming on south river: John, Peg holding
Peggy, Lou, Powell, Nancy holding baby Nancy, Lillian, and Tom Reed.
(Summer 1939)

Lillian holds her first grandchildren—Nancy Lillian Reed (4 months) and Margaret "Peggy" Musterman (4 years)—on Mother's Day. (May 1938)

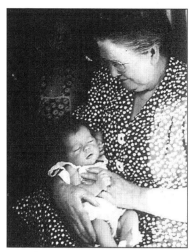

In Arlington, Virginia, Lillian holds
her granddaughter
Elizabeth Leah Reed.
(June 1942)

Lillian's seven grandchildren gather under her Christmas tree.
Peggy, Elizabeth holding Jim, Joan, Nancy, Sallie holding Jay.
(1949)

For the Annapolis Tercentenary, Lillian
made dresses for herself and granddaughter
Sallie Musterman.
(1949)

Lillian's seven grandchildren: Jim Reed, Jay Musterman,
Joan Musterman, Elizabeth Reed, Sallie Musterman,
Nancy Reed, Peggy Musterman (August 1953)

Lillian often took her grandchildren shopping on
Main Street as here with Elizabeth.
(c 1960)

Enjoying Christmas with her daughter, granddaughter,
and three great-granddaughters (Becky, Corinne,
and Dana Miller) on Christmas Day.
(1970)

Lillian's three children and Eleanor Owings, Zontian, chat with her at the surprise 90th birthday party hosted by Zonta. (1971)

With a slideshow to illustrate their "This Is Your Life" presentation, Zonta honored their last living charter member at their annual Christmas Party at the Annapolis Yacht Club.

Lillian at home in her living room.
(c 1970s)

10

THE YEARS BETWEEN
1924–1956

WHEN JOHN MUSTERMAN'S FUNERAL service was over and the graveside prayers completed, Lillian returned from the cemetery to face her future.[1] Well-meaning friends and relatives gave her "helpful" suggestions about what to do next. She rejected her sister Nan's advice: Give up the children.

Nan and Lillian, close since childhood and both milliners,[2] would often visit each other. One weekend Nan and her husband, Frank Parsons, would drive with their four children from Washington, D.C., to Annapolis; on another Lillian and John boarded the train at the West Street station with their three young ones to ride to the capital. When Lillian had gone on buying trips to New York for her hats, Nancy often had stayed in Washington with her aunt. Now, after the burial, Nan suggested—maybe even demanded—that her sister give up the children to various relatives. How could she watch them and run her business? Maybe Nan told her it was unfair to Nancy to not have a relative greet her after school. Maybe

Nan implied that "doing it all" was too much for her sister to cope with.

Lillian, as fierce as ever about keeping her family together, was furious. No. She could do it. She *would* do it. After all, she always had. Her anger at Nan was such that the sisters never spoke again.

The family grieved through the holidays, but with the new year, John, Powell, and Nancy returned to school and Lillian to her hat shop. One change occurred in the home—Nancy got a room of her own. She no longer had to sleep with her mother, as she had since they moved to Main Street. First she tried the back bedroom that had been her father's, but she decided on the tiny room over the vestibule next to the sitting room. There she had a sunny view over Main Street. Her mother let her pick out any wallpaper she liked, so Nancy chose a design of pots and pans and tea kettles. She moved her bed, vanity, chiffarobe, and a little drop-leaf desk with pearl inlay into the room. Her dresses hung in the closet down the hall.

Lillian's balancing of home and business and community activities was now even more difficult as she faced the years alone. She no longer had her husband to mind the children after school. She admonished them to play quietly and stay in the back rooms of the second floor when the store was open. They tried. They knew never to bother the customers with their noise, but some days they strayed into the sitting room. They chased one another—mostly it was the twins chasing Nancy—and made so much noise that sometimes the customers looked up from the mirrors where they were admiring themselves. When that happened, Lillian grabbed a broom and banged the handle against the store's ceiling. When the children heard those thumps, they knew their mother could hear them, and they had better settle down quickly.

After a long day, Lillian climbed the stairs to the sitting room utterly exhausted. As she sat in a chair, she loosened her shoe laces and put her aching feet on a footstool. More than once she lost her patience with the children. Nancy said, "If we spoke a cross word to our mother, she'd start crying and say, 'Do you want to put me where your father is?'"

But usually family life was smooth and manageable as it had been before the death of Mr. Musterman. The school year was filled with classes, Sunday school, Scouts, and the occasional trip to Baltimore for shopping. Lillian often hosted her Calvary Methodist's church circle in her home. Summertime meant continuing the annual visits to relatives on the Eastern Shore—her sister Abbie in Ocean City and her brother George in Onancock. Their children came to Annapolis to visit their cousins, tour the State House, and walk around the Naval Academy.

~

Sometime after 1925, Lillian had a beau for a few years. His name was William Martin Brady, and he worked at the court house on Church Circle. He was known as "one of Annapolis' finest men at the time. He was a gentleman and a wit."[3] He brightened Lillian's life for a while. They enjoyed dinners and shows and movies and friends. Some in Baltimore, some in Annapolis. The boys, now in their teens, liked him and he was good with Nancy, who was nearing the end of grammar school. Martin and Lillian took Nancy with them to see "Thurston the Great Magician"[4] at Ford's Grand Opera House in Baltimore. Lillian made Nancy a new silk dress to wear to the show. She remembered it had a navy blue top and a pleated print skirt. Lillian created the pleats by pushing the fabric through slits in a metal sheet and then pressing with a hot iron.

Thurston's touring show was as popular as the circus. Twenty or more assistants and women in flowing dresses paraded around the stage swirling streamers. Thurston was famous for levitating a woman, making a horse disappear, and sawing a person in half. Nancy was excited about the show and her new dress too.

The three of them probably sat in the front row, because Thurston picked Nancy as the lucky child to come on stage to help him. Mr. Brady came on stage too and stood nearby. As Nancy followed the magician's instructions, he told her what a great actress she was. "Finally," Nancy said, "he reached down Mr. Brady's back, and pulled out a live guinea pig, which he handed to me. Mother made me return it." During the time they were on stage, Thurston kept referring to Mr. Brady as "your daddy." This embarrassed all three, and Nancy wasn't sure if she should correct him. This awkward moment stayed with Nancy, who remembered she felt her mother's disapproval about being a spectacle. Perhaps it was that situation that began the unraveling of the relationship. Or, as one granddaughter speculated, Lillian was by now too independent to be subsumed by marriage.

As Nancy grew into her teenage years, she sometimes worked in the hat shop during the lunch hour and during sales. She helped customers, unpacked the new hats, and polished the glass cases before the season openings. A few times she went to New York and Baltimore on the buying trips. Lillian hoped her daughter would love the business and take it over one day, but Nancy had worked in the store enough to know it wasn't for her. "I couldn't stand waiting for the women to make up their minds. You know, some women try on every hat in the store," she said. Nancy dreamed of one day leaving Annapolis.

～

The twins were known as great jokesters and fun lovers, and they were truly identical, which aided in their pranks. They often exchanged roles, filling in for each other in classes, on dates, and other events. They double-dated for the high school prom, wearing different ties, to help their dates tell them apart. But halfway through the evening, they swapped ties and took each other's date home. Years later their own children often didn't know if it was their father or their uncle on the phone and sometimes called the wrong one "Daddy!" as John or Powell entered a room. At Powell's funeral, a great-niece remembered his widow saying, "I still don't know if I married the right twin."

John and Powell attended Bliss Electrical School in Takoma Park, Maryland, using funds their mother borrowed for their tuition. When they arrived that first day in 1928, their footlocker of clothes didn't—it had been shipped to Tacoma, Washington! At the end of each week, they packed up their dirty clothes and linens and mailed them to Annapolis in a canvas satchel with an Isinglass window tag that flipped back and forth to show one of two addresses. There the maid washed, ironed, and folded the items. Either Lillian or Nancy repacked the satchel and mailed it back to Bliss so that the boys had clean clothes for another week.

At Bliss, the boys encountered more "twin problems."

During exams, they sat in separate rooms to take the same final. When the papers were graded, not only did they have identical scores, but they also had missed the identical questions. They were wrongly accused of cheating.

Before graduating in 1929, both young men had jobs waiting for them. The telephone company offered John a position in its Baltimore office and Powell one in Annapolis. John and Powell stayed with AT&T through long and successful careers until retirement. Truly Ma Bell.

Sometime during the Second World War, they each had a business trip on the same day to the same place, the Naval Research Laboratory in Washington, D.C., but neither knew about the other's appointment. Powell arrived first, requested a pass, and stated his business. Sign-in was easy and he immediately received his pass. *That was quick,* he must have thought as he went to his meeting. Next, John arrived and asked for his prearranged pass. The MPs realized that an unauthorized person had it and was roaming somewhere in the building. Powell, in the middle of his meeting, suddenly was surrounded by armed guards who shoved their rifles against his chest. It was all sorted out, but after that, Powell arranged for passes in advance.

The year the boys went to Bliss—1928—Lillian together with fifteen other business women established the fifty-eighth chapter of Zonta, an international organization whose mission is to empower women. The Annapolis chapter received its charter on February 16, 1929. Each member of a Zonta chapter is the sole representative of her area of business. Thus when Lillian—who probably got the nickname "Musty"

about this time—was a member, no other milliner was permitted to join. By the time she retired in the 1960s, the number of milliners in Annapolis had shrunk from about five to zero.[5]

Zonta of Annapolis donated funds each year to the county hospital and the library. The name Mrs. Musterman often appeared in the paper as an individual sponsor of various concert series that benefited the hospital as well. Today Zonta of Annapolis offers several scholarships, advocates on various women's issues, and performs selected service initiatives, such as providing needed supplies to a women's recovery residence.

In July 1936, the year before she became Zonta's fourth president, Lillian was riding a train across the country to California. She was a delegate to the biennial Convention of Zonta, International, held that year in the elegant Mission Inn in Riverside, California. For expenses the club had given her $25.

Hers was one of the longest train rides, but stops along the way broke up the trip. At each town and city, more Zontians boarded to travel to the convention. In some towns, the train stood in the station a whole day as delegates met with local chapter members. At Salt Lake City, the Mormon Tabernacle Choir entertained the delegates after breakfast and before they toured the city. At day's end, they boarded the train and continued west. The ladies detrained at midnight in Las Vegas to visit five gambling "joints" during a one-hour stopover before arriving Friday morning in Riverside for the four-day convention that began on July 10, 1936.

When Lillian checked out of the hotel, her bill was $27.00—less than today's price for an eggs Benedict brunch in the Mission Inn's Spanish-style courtyard. Before she began her return trip, she bought a still-treasured souvenir: a large gourd pitcher with a thin gourd handle. Its hollowed-out shell of burnished ochre glistened. She knew that the blue-dotted borders and painted sailboat would be the perfect remembrance of California. At thirteen inches high and ten inches wide, it was too big to pack in her suitcase, so she must have held it in her lap like a baby as she rocked for at least four days on the return train trip to Annapolis. She placed the pitcher on the floor by her mission-style desk in the hall. It was the first thing guests saw through the railing as they climbed the steps to her second-floor sitting room. Today it graces the hearth of a granddaughter's home.

Before Lillian's trip to California, Powell married Lou Harman in June 1936.[6] John had married Margaret Patterson in 1934. Now it was Nancy's turn.

She was engaged to the midshipman she'd been dating for two years—Tom Reed from Memphis, Tennessee. Usually midshipmen are commissioned when they graduate and, at that time, newly commissioned ensigns could not marry until they had served the Navy for two years. But because of the Depression economy, the Navy was low on funds and couldn't commission all the graduates into the service. Before graduation each midshipman had to take a series of tests to determine who received a commission and became an officer and who received only a diploma. Tom "went out on his eyes" is how Nancy always explained it—he failed the eye test and could not be commissioned. A new vision chart—different from the one Tom had memorized each year to remain in the

Academy—was used to test the graduating midshipmen that year. Lillian hosted three of Tom's brothers and wives during June Week in the rooms she usually rented to families of graduating midshipmen. Tom received his Bachelor of Science degree in June 1936 and had a job waiting in Philadelphia for about $25 a week. Now that he was a civilian, he and Nancy did not have to wait two years to marry.

The couple's September wedding was officiated by a Methodist minister in Lillian's living room. John and Powell and their wives, as well as Nancy's friend Dorothy Hawkins and the minister, gathered around the fireplace where Nancy had once played with her dolls. Now it was draped in greenery and flowers that flowed from mantel to floor. Tom was in a suit and Nancy was all in green—shoes, hose, crepe traveling suit with a beautifully embroidered soutache jacket, and a perky green hat. Nancy often said she always hated that hat, but her mother chose it, so she wore it on the train and in New York where they honeymooned.

～

Now that the children were married, Lillian remodeled the house on Main Street for the last time. She created a second-floor apartment for Powell and Lou, and eventually their children. She installed a sink, refrigerator, and stove in Nancy's room to create a kitchen—the wallpaper of pots and pans chosen years before worked just fine. The rest of the floor remained the same. For herself, she turned the first-floor kitchen and dining room (on the common wall with the store) into a studio apartment. When in the mid-1950s Powell's family moved to a new house in Homewood, just a few miles away, Lillian moved upstairs to live until she needed the care of a nursing home. During that time, she leased the first-floor studio and the third-floor, one-bedroom apartment to tenants.

The years flew by. Grandchildren were born—by 1950 she had seven in all[7]—and the business flourished. Friends called her "Musty," nieces and nephews called her "Aunt Lil" or "Aunt Lillian"—Lill-*yan*, not Lill-y-ann. To her grandchildren she was "Gran." For many Christmases Lillian's home was full of her children and grandchildren sharing food, gifts, and laughter.

The fond memories of her adoring grandchildren are many. Powell's children Sallie and Jay were right in town and visited whenever they wanted. The other granddaughters loved spending a week in the summer with "their Gran." A visit by John's daughter Peggy actually made the newspaper.[8] When Nancy's family lived in Philadelphia, Lillian stopped to visit for a few days on her way back from New York. She would take one or the other granddaughter on the steam train to Baltimore and then the electric train to Annapolis to stay for a week. Young Nancy was fascinated seeing her grandmother "take out her teeth and put them in a glass" by her bed every night.

All her granddaughters loved working in the store with their grandmother, especially in late summer when the boxes arrived filled with new season's hats. They pulled them out, tried them on, and pranced around the store before tagging them and hiding them in a drawer.

The grandsons weren't quite as enthralled with the hat shop as the granddaughters. Jim, the youngest grandchild, told of his grandmother taking him behind the counter and asking him to hold out his hands. His eyes grew large as she opened the cash drawer, scooped out all the pennies from their wooden bin (she never had a cash register), and filled his outstretched hands. He was rich! Rather than stay in the store, he preferred walking up and down Main Street when he visited. As soon as possible, he headed to the pawn shop across the street to gaze at the knives, guns, and handcuffs in the window. "That pawn shop was like forbidden fruit and edgy. Maybe the antithesis of a ladies' millinery shop," he said.

Jay remembered that when he was a toddler and his family still lived in the second-floor apartment, he would sneak downstairs at night to crawl into bed with his grandmother. Later, when he was a teen, they'd walk to Little Campus Inn (now Galway Bay Irish Restaurant and Pub) to enjoy the chicken basket together. They often went to movies at the Circle Movie Theatre.

Lillian listened to her grandchildren's sorrows and wiped away their tears. When Sallie called, pouring out her troubles about something that happened at school or with her friends or family, her Gran always said, "Come on down, let's play Canasta and talk about it." Lillian was an avid Canasta player and taught all her grandchildren the game.

She was generous at Christmas and gave each grandchild not only a present but a $25 U.S. Savings Bond to save until they went to college. At family gatherings, she was known to slip one, and then another, a dollar when the others weren't looking, and say, "Don't tell." Each grandchild believed they were their Gran's favorite.

In early December 1946, Lillian received terrible news. Her oldest granddaughter, Peggy, was stricken with polio. She was ten years old and spent the next four months hospitalized. Only a few visitors were allowed by her bedside and only on

Sundays between 2 p.m. and 4 p.m. But Lillian boarded the train or rode with Powell to Baltimore after church to sit by Peggy and chat about many things, including ballet and religion. Sallie remembered visiting and thinking how sad it was to see her cousin so ill.

Peggy was strong willed and determined, just like her grandmother. She recovered, came home with crutches, and returned to school having missed almost a year. However, her illness severely weakened one leg, which meant that the long staircase to her grandmother's sitting room above the store was now a challenge. She told her Aunt Nancy years later that when she and the family arrived at the entrance hall, she'd look up to the top of the staircase, and think, *That's a mountain I have to go up every time I come visit Gran.*

Annapolis celebrated its Tercentenary in May 1949 with a week full of events.[9] Some for children, others for adults. A garden party at Reynolds Tavern, a pageant at Sandy Point. Many Annapolitans dressed in colonial clothing for the events.[10] Lillian made floral-patterned dresses and hats for herself and Mrs. Kashner to wear in the store as well as an outfit for her granddaughter Sallie. They probably wore their outfits to watch a celebratory parade go up Main Street. Sallie still treasures the picture of herself with her grandmother in their beautiful colonial hats and dresses. It hangs in her hallway today.

Nancy's family never lived in Maryland after she married. When World War II began, the need for servicemen was desperate and Tom Reed, even with his bad eyesight, was accepted as a reserve officer. After the war, he made the Navy his career. The family lived the Navy life, moving from place to place every two or three years.[11] As they traveled to new homes, the family always stayed a week or two with Lillian. And she stayed a week or so with them at each duty station except London. Out-of-town visitors to Annapolis often earned a mention in a brief social note in the *Evening Capital*, as when Nancy and Tom were in town in 1953: "Fourteen Gather for Musterman Reunion."[12] The whole family enjoyed a crab feast on her spacious back porch before Nancy's family was off to London for two years.

The years between her husband's death and her children becoming adults with families of their own were fairly uneventful times for Lillian and her business. She survived the occasional setback, as when Hurricane Hazel ripped through Annapolis.

That night she certainly was up listening to the roaring winds. It started on October 15, 1954, at about 5 p.m., just as she was closing the store. The winds reached eighty-eight miles per hour. No power. No telephone service. Trees came crashing down. Water flooded beyond City Dock all the way up Main Street to Francis Street. The descriptions of the damage ranged from roofs blown off to flooded living rooms and kitchens. When morning dawned, Lillian saw the results of all the clatter of the night: the wreckage of both back porches. She had them rebuilt and was grateful the store wasn't damaged as well.[13]

The store itself was damaged sometime later in the 1950s. A driver trying to park in front of her house must have hit the accelerator a bit too hard. The car jumped the curb and crashed against the store's foundation, shattering her plate-glass display window. Historic Annapolis, Inc.,[14] whose goal was preservation of old Annapolis architecture, suggested she install a storefront with rows of little panes framed in white mullions. They wanted her store to look a bit more colonial. Lillian certainly listened and considered for a moment before pointing out that if she had little framed windows, "people won't be able to see my hats." The new display window was installed, identical to the original of 1921.[15]

Sometime after the window was replaced, Lillian smelled an odd scent rising from the basement below. She called the fire department, which quickly "quenched" the "oil burner flare-up." The *Evening Capital* noted "no damage was reported" at L.P. Musterman's.[16]

But six months later, "no damage" at 197 Main Street was not the front-page story about Musterman's Hat Shop.

11

FIRE!

A SIX-COLUMN-WIDE HEADLINE SCREAMED AT readers: "15 Routed As Flames Damage Main Street Shops." Fire trucks with ladders stretched to the rooftops were pictured across three columns. The subheading told the rest: "Residents of Apartments Forced to Flee In Early Hours As Flames Spread." Another subheading added more drama: "Trapped Fireman Rescued From Building Ledge." That was the front page of the *Evening Capital* on Wednesday afternoon, April 24, 1957.[1]

On the Tuesday after Easter, Lillian went to bed as usual. Business had been slow, as the spring rush was over. She soaked her aching feet after dinner, took a bath, and slept soundly in her bedroom in the second-floor apartment above the store. The temperatures were unusually mild, in the eighties in the daytime and never dipping below sixty degrees all night. The humidity high, typical for Annapolis.

By 5 a.m. she was awake. Maybe she smelled smoke or heard the firefighters banging on her door. The first alarm had gone out at 4:45 a.m. Lillian moved quickly. She shoved her feet into slippers by the bed; grabbed her bathrobe, glasses, and purse; and fled together with the tenants, Katherine

M. Kibler and Reida Longanecker. A firefighter led them out of the building and across Main Street, where they stood in front of the Capital Restaurant. They watched flames roar up, smoke pour out, and water from the firefighters' hoses swamp her store.

Soon her son, Powell pulled his car to the curb. Lillian climbed into the back seat and huddled with her granddaughter Sallie behind Powell and Lou, his wife. (Their son Jay was in the hospital for hernia surgery.) They sat helpless as firefighters followed the blaze up Main Street. Sallie was horrified as she watched flames brighten the early morning sky and smoke billow up. She couldn't believe such a thing could happen to her grandmother, that her store might be destroyed.

Trucks and firefighters from the three closest stations arrived first—Waterwitch Hook and Ladder, Independent, and the Rescue Hose companies. Fifteen minutes later three more units joined the battle: Eastport, West Annapolis, and Naval Academy. They sped through the city streets with alarms blaring and lights flashing. Main Street was impassable.

Lillian certainly clutched her purse and fretted. With no time to put her hair up in a tidy bun, wispy gray streams flowed down her back. For such a fastidious lady, this must have been embarrassing. Suddenly she remembered her dentures. "Powell, go in and get my teeth," she said. Powell, who knew just about everyone in town and was a second cousin to a police detective, got out of the car and talked to one of the firemen who was taking a break. The fire was no longer a danger to 197 Main Street, so they went into the house and up to her second-floor bedroom while chaos continued in the buildings farther up the street. They soon returned with her dentures.

According to a fire inspector, the blaze started in the rear of the hat shop, quickly climbed the partition with Rainbow Cleaners next door, and filled the attic. From there flames spread through the attics of 201 and 203 Main Street and down into the apartments below—the ones above the stores. Perhaps an iron was left on in the work area. Lillian shuddered for years afterward wondering if she caused the devastation.

As smoke and fire poured through the ceiling into the apartment above the cleaners, it forced James M. Collins, his wife, and five children out. Cynthia Collins was seven years old at the time. She clutched her dolly tight to her chest as she was led down the steep, wooden outdoor stairs at the back of the house. "We lost everything in that fire. But we had each other," she said. The damage was so extensive, the family never returned.[2]

As if this wasn't enough drama to start an April day, the crowd watching from the sidewalk looked up to see a firefighter climb out a window on the third floor above the cleaners. He lay on the ledge as flames flared behind him. He'd been searching the front room just as fire broke through the ceiling and cut him off. As quickly as they could, firefighters maneuvered a hook and ladder truck to the building and raised the ladder to him. He was able to climb down to safety.

When the fire was extinguished and the fire trucks drove away, Lillian learned that although her store had escaped the flames, her building suffered water and smoke damage. Fire had reached the third floors of the next three buildings—199, 201, and 203 Main Street—while smoke and water had damaged their second floors. The fire never reached Eggleston's Jewelers at 205 Main Street, but five people[3] who lived in various apartments above the jewelers' were evacuated to escape the smoke. That building and Ryan Stationers at 207 sustained only water and smoke damage.

The stock in L.P. Musterman's was a disaster. Some of the store fittings were damaged. A friend said to her years later: "I can still see the pathetic remains of the window draperies and curtains. You were certain your career had come to an end."[4]

But although she was seventy-five, Lillian Musterman's career had not come to an end. Not yet.

Perhaps not giving up no matter what was second nature by now for Lillian. Perhaps a new challenge invigorated her just when others would gladly retire. Perhaps her granddaughter Sallie was an influence. She urged her grandmother to wait to retire until "I'm old enough to take over" the millinery store.

Being a naturally resilient person, Lillian went right to work. Her friends and family encouraged her and she obtained the loans necessary to repair the damage. Her spirits were buoyed. Although all of her spring models were ruined and the building badly damaged, she began making plans to refurbish the store. In May she sent a letter to the editor of the *Evening Capital* thanking the fire department for their efforts[5] and placed an ad in the paper: "I expect to resume my business about August 1957."[6]

She selected the fabrics, paint, and flooring. Again it would be a bright room designed to set off her hats to their best advantage. The cases she had bought in the 1920s and the huge wooden drawers that held those hats not on display were still usable, as was the gilt Rococo mirror. The only change she made was to add an air conditioning unit. Other than that, the store looked just as it always had.

By August 15, 1957—less than four months after the fire—L.P. Musterman's had its second grand opening. Lillian stated her philosophy to a reporter: "nothing is impossible if you really want to do it." [7]

The store was so crowded with baskets and bouquets of flowers sent to her for the reopening that her faithful clients—some of whom were customers for more than thirty years—could hardly get near the new hats. The paper reported, "Mrs. Musterman laughed, 'I can't decide whether I'm selling flowers, or hats.' She explained happily that her opening day had brought her more business than any other day in her thirty-eight years of selling fashionable chapeaus to Annapolitans." [8]

Even the Shady Side news column noted that:

> ... patrons ... were pleased to enter the doors ... Feeling just a bit afraid that they would lose this lovely place after the fire, they felt a sense of relief ... to know that Mrs. Musterman will continue to carry a line of millinery satisfactory to all. [9]

One of her customers remarked: "After I look around and see what Musty's done, I don't think anything's impossible." [10]

12

LAST WALTZ

*B*Y THE 1960S, ALTHOUGH hats could be found toward the back of some clothing stores, L.P. Musterman Hat Shop was the only millinery in town.[1] Changes occurring in American society at the time took hold by the late 1960s, but early in the decade women still wore hats. And Lillian was still there offering the latest styles to the women of Annapolis. Religious services, Easter, luncheons, teas, weddings—all were occasions for a new hat.

She was still busy with family too. She attended most of her grandchildren's weddings and held with joy her great-grandchildren in the ensuing years. She lent support and sympathy to her granddaughter Nancy, widowed too young with an infant and a toddler to raise alone. While her daughter and some grandchildren lived in other states, those who lived nearby visited her regularly in her store or on her back porch.

Annapolis activities also occupied her free time. She regularly attended Zonta and other organizational meetings. She was a benefactor of the Fine Arts Committee that formed in the early 1960s under the leadership of Beth Whaley.[2, 3] When the committee published the booklet *Annapolis Faces*, Lillian's was featured among its pages.[4] Her picture with Mayor Joseph

H. Griscom, Sr., made the front page of the *Evening Capital* in 1961. He is shown presenting her a floral arrangement in appreciation of her store's being the first of thirteen businesses on upper Main Street to complete exterior renovations. This was part of a self-help renewal and revitalization program going on in Annapolis at a time when, according to a later mayor, Pip Moyer, thirteen businesses on Main Street were closed.[5]

One night in 1963, as Lillian was reading in bed, she casually dropped her hand to her chest. She felt a hard pealike lump. Her doctor gave her the dreaded diagnosis: breast cancer. After surgery and convalescence, she returned to the store within a few months. Although she was eighty-two, even cancer didn't force her into retirement.

But teased hair and bouffant hairstyles did.

While some still wore a hat for religious occasions, changing fashions and relaxation of social expectations meant only few women continued to believe a covered head was required. Lillian realized millinery was a business of the past and her advancing years told her it was time to slow down. When the announcement appeared in the paper, those who loved to go to L.P. Musterman's Hat Shop couldn't believe the news: Musterman's was closing. After the spring season in 1967, a final sale emptied the store of hats and at eighty-seven Lillian retired.

"Mrs. Musterman's Gift," a seven-verse poem, appeared in the paper in June.[6] Sigrid Theobald began with "Sir: There's a shop that's closed on Main Street / That's thrived for many years … ." It went on: "Many hats will linger / On many closet shelves / But the warmest glow to last / Will be her smile within ourselves."

When the last sale was over and the curtains were drawn over the display window, Lillian locked the door, walked a few steps, and climbed the stairs to her apartment over the store. Never again would a customer sit on the velvet bench in front of the gilt mirror and glance up to see the reflection of that old gray head shake back and forth or hear "that hat won't do." No young lady or matron would turn her head this way and that as Lillian cocked a brim or fluffed a veil. Never again will visitors to downtown Annapolis gaze at a display of hats in the store window of 197 Main Street.

As the years went by, passersby witnessed a number of stores come and go at 197 Main Street. In the late 1960s and 1970s, the window displayed a variety of "new age" items when Kaleidoscope followed by the Charisma Shop rented the space. Next kilts and Waterford crystal beckoned customers to enter and buy from Scottish and Irish Imports. The 1990s brought Interior Concepts, which stayed into the early 2000s. The interior decorators used the upstairs rooms as design studios and made a showroom of the store. They filled it with upholstered sofas, casual chairs, and occasional tables and lamps. The walls displayed fine art and drapery samples. Creative décor—pillows, footstools, statues, bric-a-brac—added color and filled every shelf and table. During the holidays a floor-to-ceiling tree loaded with artistic ornaments enticed customers. Chef's Revenge was the last occupant. Where hats of all colors and fabrics had once surrounded customers, unique kitchen utensils, fine cooking pots and pans, and skillets of all sizes—almost exclusively red and white—took their place.

Although these businesses offered no hats (except for some Scottish tam o'shanters and perhaps a chef's toque), the same store interior that Lillian Musterman had designed in 1921 remained. Some people, especially her grandchildren, wandered in occasionally and looked at the ever-changing merchandise, but all the while they remembered the woman and her hats. By the Christmas season of 2008, the Chef's Revenge was gone and the Maryland Federation of Art filled the walls with works of local artists. But by New Year's the store was vacant.

Renovations began. Renovations stopped. Brown paper went up on the display window, hiding the destruction of the interior as remodeling continued. It looked like Lillian's preparations before a season opening. Nothing happened for a couple of years.

The new building owners, Joseph Shyue-Hae and Jane Yu-Chen Jiau, were expanding into the hat shop from 195 Main Street, which they had owned since 1995.[7] After the wall separating the two buildings was broken through, what had been L.P. Musterman's hat shop became the main dining room and sushi bar of Joss. All that remains of Lillian's hat shop is the large glass display window and the glass door. To-day, rather than hats, red Japanese lanterns call to customers walking on Main Street.[8]

When she closed her business in 1967, Lillian took her hand mirrors, African violets, and the Degas print "The Millinery Shop." For the next fourteen years she lived above the store. Her visitors rang the doorbell and then stepped back to the sidewalk to catch the key she dropped out her kitchen window. They enjoyed a lunch of cold cuts from Rookie's Delicatessen in her tiny kitchen or joined her for an iced tea on her grand back porch. There she continued to host family get-togethers. She attended Zonta meetings and Eastern Star events as well as occasionally hosting her church circle. Friends gave her rides to Sunday services at Calvary Methodist on State Circle and later to its new building on Rowe Boulevard. She attended many celebrations of family and friends—christenings, graduations, weddings, and funerals—throughout her remaining years.

As she entertained in her living room, Lillian's hands were still busy but now her arthritic fingers were no longer nimble and her eyesight was dimming. She'd pick up a deck of cards to play solitaire as she chatted. Age brought her new challenges in the form of typical health problems—high blood pressure, arthritis, cataracts, and gall bladder pain.

Shortly after her ninetieth birthday in December 1971, the Annapolis chapter of Zonta honored Lillian—Musty—at their annual Christmas Party. The Annapolis Yacht Club was filled with her children, old friends, a shop assistant, a former millinery salesman, and Zontians. Even the Feldmeyer family, so instrumental in her life, was represented. She was completely surprised when Eleanor Owings turned to her and said: "Musty, you are our loved one! … and here is your life!" [9]

As Ms. Owings narrated, the evening became one of memories shared with and by friends and family. Stories and photographs, tales of humor and pathos, recalled Lillian's life from her girlhood up to that evening's celebration. As the event drew to a close, Eleanor Owings said:

Yours has been a unique life, Musty, full of love and

laughter, sorrow and joy, ambition and its fulfillment, difficulties overcome and the love and admiration of many more people than you, perhaps, realize.

~

Lillian continued to live in her home for another six years until one day she fell and broke her leg. She lay in pain for hours near the door of her bedroom unable to reach her phone and call for help. It was clear that living alone in her apartment was now unwise. After much deliberation and weighing of alternatives, the best she and her family could arrange was a shared room at the Bay Ridge Nursing and Convalescent Home in the Eastport section of Annapolis. There she lived out her remaining years.

She brought a few dresses, a couple pieces of jewelry, and some personal items. On her new dresser she placed the two pictures from her chest of drawers at home: one of her husband with her twin boys taken in 1910 and one of herself with the boys and baby daughter taken in 1916. They soon were joined by more pictures of her children, grandchildren, and great-grandchildren. Her apartment furnishings, heirlooms, and antiques were distributed among family members; what was left was sold. The building also was sold. What John and Lillian Musterman bought in 1921 for $6,000 went for $140,000 in 1976.

At the nursing home, Lillian joined in all the activities: church services on Sunday in the day room, bingo during the week, and being entertained by various groups that came to cheer up the residents. A few of her old friends lived there too. One was a member of her church circle—Myrtle Young, who once lived a couple blocks away on Conduit Street. Now they were a hall away. When he was a teenager, Lillian's son John had saved Mrs. Young's daughter, Ruby, from drowning. The two old women enjoyed the visits of the three great-grand-daughters they shared.[10]

Soon after Lillian moved in, a woman called out from her room, "Lillian Musterman is here! That's her laugh." At the nursing home everyone called her Mrs. Musterman, and she was as popular as ever, so much so that she was elected the Queen of Mother's Day. Again her picture appeared in the *Evening Capital.*[11]

In her remaining years, Lillian read a bit, although her sight was limited to one eye. Her fingers became severely arthritic. She lived at that nursing home until she was ninety-eight. She quietly succumbed to a slow-growing cancer on April 5, 1980,[12] eight months before her ninety-ninth birthday.

In early 1978, Mary Felter, a local Annapolis writer, interviewed Lillian at the nursing home.[13] She explained her circumstances as Ms. Felter sat by her bedside: "I had to give up everything—this is all I have [a bed in a shared room]."

Ms. Felter said, "Your hat store must have been very important to you."

Lillian replied: "It was my life."

Before Ms. Felter turned off the tape recorder and began her goodbyes, she asked: "What was it like when you started in business? Was it unusual for a woman to run a shop by herself? Did you consider yourself liberated? You seem like an independent lady."

Lillian didn't hesitate in her response:

I had to work too hard to think about being liberated. I had to be [independent]. I was in business by myself, not with my husband … very unusual to run a shop by yourself.

I'm a waltzer. I feel I should still waltz.

Appendix A

WHO WERE THOSE MUSTERMANS?

OHANN HEINRICH MUSTERMANN[1] WAS probably about thirty years old when his ship silently slipped into the Port of Baltimore.[2] Few were on the docks to greet the passengers. He, like many German immigrants, debarked onto the piers of Fell's Point, the women first with great bundles on their scarfed heads and carrying straw hampers. Few had trunks. Next came the men in wooden shoes and workmen's caps. All were herded into pens for health examinations: first their eyes for trachoma, a contagious eye disease; next their scalps; and then the rest of their bodies. Most passed. Most were fed while they waited to board trains to all parts of the United States. Those like Johann Mustermann who would remain in Baltimore were sent to a separate pen for inspections. Once fed, they could walk into the city to seek temporary housing.[3]

Johann, the first Musterman in Annapolis, Maryland, immigrated to the United States sometime after the German revolutions of 1848 failed and their achievements, including the "Basic Rights for the German People," had been dissolved. Many others also left the Germanic states—bakers, coopers, joiners, upholsterers, shoemakers, seamstresses, tanners, brewers, carpenters, smiths, masons, weavers, retailers, tailors, and glazers. Farmers by the thousands moved away after suffering severe crop failures. Men chose to cross the Atlantic Ocean rather than be forced into the army. Families sought safety because of religious conflicts. Some wanted greater civic and political freedoms. All came for better opportunities. Johann was most likely a poor farmer, and that perhaps is what prompted him to board a ship in Bremen and sail to Baltimore, Maryland—alone. There he was hoping to find opportunity.

A "Johan Musterman" [*sic*] appears in "Maryland, Baltimore Passenger Lists," as immigrating in 1853. His place of birth is listed as Neuenkirchen, but no birthdate is included.[4] Family records list this first Johann Heinrich Mustermann as born on July 28, 1821, in the area or village of Gehrde, Bersenbrück, in the Electorate or Kingdom of Hannover (now the state of Lower Saxony), Germany.[5, 6]

Neuenkirchen is also a village in Lower Saxony less than ten miles from Gehrde.[7] At the time Johann left his home— maybe first to stay in Neuenkirchen before boarding his ship in Bremen—Gehrde was a tiny village of self-reliant and free craftworkers, such as tobacco spinners, dyers, bakers, yarn buyers, and cattle merchants. In feudal times, the common people had little land that they could cultivate, and nearly all country dwellers "belonged" to the land-owning lord (were they serfs?). Following the Thirty Years War and two hundred years before Johann emigrated, the population grew so much that people had to live in barns, bakehouses (outdoor kitchens), and turf huts. In the early 1800s, movement from place to place required registration with the police. When that restriction was lifted and economic conditions improved somewhat, emigration to the United States became feasible. Literally thousands left the Gehrde region over the next hundred years, and Johann Heinrich Mustermann was one of them.[8]

As Johann and his fellow passengers climbed the gangplank of a wooden, three-masted vessel, they were looked upon as not much better than ship's cargo. Over one hundred people descended to ladders to the steerage, which just a week before would have been used to stow coffee, rice, tobacco, cotton, and other goods being shipped from America to Europe. The emigrants brought their own bedding. They slept five to a berth. They cooked their own food. They cleaned their own small area of the dark, belowdecks living quarters. Sometimes water was rationed to eight or nine ounces a day. The voyage took about forty-five days, but stormy weather or lack of wind to fill the sails could make the crossing of the Atlantic Ocean last sixty days. Food—usually salted meat, herring, potatoes, rice, dried peas, and bread—was often spoiled before a schooner even weighed anchor.

Once in Baltimore, Johann had an English name—John Henry Musterman—but most likely his new German friends continued to call him Johann. In 1853 he was living in the Fell's Point area of Baltimore at "Columbia House," on the southeast corner of Eastern Avenue and President Street.[9] This was probably one of the many immigrant houses operated by religious and charitable organizations at that time. In those years, so many German immigrants lived in Baltimore—20,000 in 1850—that more than twenty churches held services in that language, and public school classes were taught in German in many immigrant neighborhoods.

Johann stayed in Baltimore for an unknown amount of time, then packed his few personal items in a wooden footlocker, still with its Bremen sticker on it, and headed to Annapolis. That footlocker serves as a coffee table in one of Lillian's great-granddaughters' homes today. Though torn and tattered, the sticker remains.

Why Annapolis? Perhaps he knew of the vibrant German community on the outskirts of town. Or that Germans directly immigrated to Annapolis since Colonial days. Maybe mutual friends in Germany had given him letters of introduction. He might have had a position arranged before he left the old country. Johann could have known or known of the Feldmeyers, Rehns, and Westphals as well as other Germans living there. Those three families would be tied together with the Mustermans by partnerships and marriages for years to come.

The Feldmeyer family was the most prominent of these families. The patriarch, Gottlieb, a blacksmith and carriage maker, had arrived in Annapolis in 1844. He eventually bought the Gassaway house at 194 Prince George Street and filled it with his many children.[10] That home is where John Henry Musterman (Johann's son) and Lillian Powell Johnson met. After he retired, Gottlieb lived at 104 Prince George Street, leaving the large home at 194 Prince George Street to his single children and grandchildren.[11]

After settling in Annapolis, Johann met Anna Catharina Rehn, another German immigrant. Her family may have arrived in Baltimore on August 31, 1837, when Annie (as she was known) was ten years old.[12] Their ship was the *Gustav* and it had sailed from Bremen. The family was from the town of Marburg in Hesse, where Annie Rehn was born. It is today considered one of the best examples of a medieval hilltown. Marburg survived World War II basically intact because it was designated a "hospital city" for wounded German soldiers. What bombing it did experience was generally limited to the railways. The streets of residences and shops travel down toward the oldest Protestant university in Germany (founded 1527) and the river Lahn. Many Mustermanns lived in Marburg in post-World War II times, indicating a branch of Johann's family may have lived there at the time he left Gehrde for America.[13]

In Annapolis, Annie's father, Louis H. Rehn, had a dry goods and clothing store at the foot of Main Street at City Dock. The family lived farther up the street at 149. When the city celebrated the bicentennial of its charter in 1908, the business was described in a special edition of the paper.[14] Of Louis H. Rehn (Annie's brother or nephew), purveyor of dry goods, notions, and clothing, it was written:

> Among merchants here none is more willingly given a first place than Mr. Louis H. Rehn ... [who] keeps on hand constantly a most extensive stock of dry goods, hosiery, notions, carpets, mattings, oil cloths, men's, ... waists, corsets, fancy goods ...

Johann and Annie married in 1856, and soon thereafter, they were living on West Street, where many other German immigrants lived—Ellinghusens and Engelkes, Muhlmeisters and Schaulbs, plus many more listed in the *Annapolis City*

Directory.[15] In 1870 about 170 Germans lived in Annapolis. [16] They filled a full range of occupations—blacksmiths, carpenters, painters, builders, clerks, haulers, bakers, and barkeeps. Many other German immigrants had farms and homes scattered along both sides of West Street, beyond the National Cemetery, in the area known then and now as Germantown.[17] There members of the German community gathered for social events, meetings of the German society to preserve the culture, and maybe even enjoyed a polka or two. Johann and his family most likely did too. They certainly went to the unveiling of Baron Johann de Kalb's statue on the State House grounds to honor the Revolutionary war hero who was as German as they were.[18]

The inner West Street "Germantown suburb" of Annapolis ran from about 165 West Street to about 181 West Street. St. Martin's Lutheran Church, which held services in German until 1916, was a short walk away on Francis Street.[19] When the Mustermans first moved to West Street, the road was dirt and often muddy. By 1910, it was paved with bricks.

Johann and Annie Musterman soon had a family of three girls and three boys. Only the first three children survived into the new century: Catharine Elizabeth (1857–1932), John Henry (1859–1924—Lillian's husband), and Andrew Hermann (1862–1952). After Johann died in 1879, Annie Musterman ran a corner grocery/candy store in the front room of 137 Conduit Street. The corner of the house is angled so that the door faces the intersection of Conduit with Union Street. Many small groceries and confectioneries throughout Annapolis designed their entrances this way. Annie lived in the other rooms of the house with her daughter's family, the

Westphals, while her son John Musterman—a bachelor into his forties—occupied the upstairs attic.

~

John Musterman's sister Lizzie (Catharine Elizabeth) married John William Henry Westphal. He had left Germany in 1857, sailed the world on a merchant ship, and settled in Annapolis in 1870, six years before they married.[20] He was a painter at the Naval Academy when they met. Lizzie managed her mother's grocery/candy store as well as raised her family of six living children at 137 Conduit Street. By the mid-1920s, their son William Henry was a blacksmith living at 9 Dean Street with his family.[21] Another son, Harry, also a blacksmith, lived at 102 Charles Street. Lizzie's daughter Ruby, a notary public, together with her husband John Waters Chaney, who owned a livery, and their son Jack lived at 137 Conduit Street.[22]

In the 1930s the Chaney family, together with Lizzie, moved to a larger home on Thompson Street.[23] Because of the twenty-year age difference between Lillian and her husband John Musterman, his nieces and nephews were close in age to Lillian. His niece, Ruby Westphal Chaney, became her close friend.

John's brother Andrew Musterman was a railroad fireman and later a machinist at the Naval Academy.[24] He and his wife Catherine Amelia had seven children—one of them named John Henry Musterman II.[25] Andrew is noted to be an engineer in the 1910 *Annapolis City Directory*, living at 179 West Street. It must have been a huge house, because the 1924 *Annapolis City Directory* lists Andrew Musterman (his wife Amelia was by then deceased) and all his living children and their spouses at this address: John Henry Musterman (clerk) and his wife Helen Litz, Catherine and her husband Robert Zindorf, Andrew Jesse Musterman (clerk, Hotel Maryland) and his wife Bertha Lee[26] (who later lived on Munroe Court), and James Musterman (clerk) and his wife Hilda Lee. According to the Musterman family tree (based on Andrew Jesse Musterman's genealogy data), four children under four years of age were living there too.

That the families were close in both affection and distance is evidenced by the annual ritual of Christmas gift exchanges. During the 1920s, Nancy Musterman (daughter of John and Lillian) and her cousin Jack Chaney (son of Ruby and Waters) filled his little red wagon with Christmas presents their mothers had wrapped and pulled it around Annapolis, as her twin brothers had done in earlier years. They made deliveries to all their Musterman aunts and uncles and cousins. After Nancy met Jack at his house at Union and Conduit, they headed over to West Street to their Uncle Andrew's and visited with all the folks who lived there—Mustermans and Zindorfs. Then they'd head back down West Street, still dragging that wagon, taking gifts to even more cousins in the William and Maude Westphal family on Dean Street. Next up to Cathedral and over to Charles Street to arrive at the Harry Westphal family home on the corner. Most likely they visited even more folks along the route before they finally returned to the candy store.

∽

Many of the homes along West Street, beginning at Colonial Avenue (numbers 165 through 181), including that of Andrew and Catherine Musterman at 179, fell into disrepair in the late 1990s. They were set for demolition in May 2000 when the city approved $8 million to make way for the Cecil and Martha Knighton Facility. On the corner of West Street and Colonial Avenue, Ramsey's Music and a warehouse were destroyed, but fortunately the Historic Annapolis Foundation intervened. HAF appealed to the City Council and literally stopped the wrecking ball.[27] Mayor Dean Johnson appointed a citizen's group to guide the design process for the Knighton complex. The current (2020) Annapolis mayor Gavin Buckley and owner of the buildings proposed a plan to retain the streetscape on West Street and shield the garage from view. The committee recommended that the buildings become a buffer for the garage.[28, 29]

The design was approved after Ellen Moyer became mayor in December 2001. With Mr. Knighton she cut the ribbon and opened the garage in November 2004.[30, 31]

Today (summer 2019), the once vacant lot on the corner of Colonial Avenue and West Street provides outside dining for Lemongrass Thai at 167. The high-end Metropolitan Kitchen and Lounge at 169 extends through four former homes from its entrance at 175. A business occupies 177, once the lodgings shared by a bricklayer, carpenter, and plasterer. And a trendy salon combines two former homes at 179 and 181.[32] Those last three structures with their original gabled roofs still provide a visual memory, recalling a time when many families lived on West Street in the early 1900s, including the Andrew and Catherine Musterman family at 179.

The Children and Grandchildren of John Henry Musterman, Annapolis, Maryland[33]

Note: The complete genealogy containing six generations is not provided here to protect the privacy of living persons.

John Henry Musterman
> b. 28 July 1821 Gehrde, Bersenbrück, Hannover, Germania
> d. about 31 Oct 1870 Annapolis, MD

married on 11 Dec 1856 to

Anna Catharina Rehn
> b. 9 Oct 1827 Marburg, Hessen, Germania
> d. 10 Jan 1893 Baltimore, MD

They had six children (all births and deaths in Annapolis, Maryland):

- Catharine Elizabeth Musterman
  > b. 5 Jan 1857   d. 23 Apr 1932
- John Henry Musterman
  > b. 13 Aug 1859   d. 23 Dec 1924
- Andrew Hermann Musterman
  > b. 2 Mar 1862   d. 11 Nov 1952
- Margaret Musterman
  > b. 28 Apr 1865   d. 6 Jun 1865
- Maria Catharine Musterman
  > b. 28 Aug 1866   d. 10 Jan 1893
- Louis Henry Musterman
  > b. 10 Oct 1869   d. 11 Jul 1887

Catharine Elizabeth Musterman (1857–1932) and John Henry William Westphal (1841–1928)

Catharine Elizabeth Musterman (1857–1932) b: 05 Jun 1857, d: 23 Apr 1932 in Annapolis, MD
   married on 23 Aug 1876 to
John Henry William Westphal (1841–1928) b: 26 Jul 1841 in Altona, a suburb of Hamburg, Germany. d: 27 Nov 1928 in Annapolis, MD
   They had seven children:

   William Henry Westphal (1878–1950) b: 18 Jan 1878, d: 10 Sep 1950
   married on 26 Dec. 1899 to
   Maude Rawlings (1873–1963) b: 04 Mar 1873, d: 29 Jul 1963
   They had five children.

   Catherine Henrietta Westphal (1880–unk) b: 24 Jun 1880

   Emma Westphal (1882–unk) b: 23 Oct 1882
   married on 29 Jan 1913 to
   Emmett Fordyce
   They had no issue.

   Elsie May Westphal (1886–1945) b: 11 Jul 1886, d: 23 Dec 1945
   married on 11 Jul 1905 to
   Joseph Mackinnon
   They had five children.

Rosetta Westphal

Ruby Matilda Westphal (1892–1978) b: 10 Sep 1892,
  d: 04 Sep 1978 in Annapolis, MD
married on 21 Mar 1917 in Annapolis, MD to
John Waters Chaney d: Annapolis, MD
  They had one child.

Louis Westphal (1899–1906) b: 23 Sep 1899, d: 20 Feb
  1906

Andrew Hermann Musterman (1862–1952) and Catherine Amelia Smith (1873–1905)

Andrew Hermann Musterman (1862–1952) b: 02 Mar
  1862, d: 11 Nov 1952
  married on 06 Sep 1893 to
Catherine Amelia Smith (1873–1905) b: 13 Apr 1873,
  d: 01 Oct 1905
  They had seven children:

John Henry Musterman II (1895–1975) b: 21 May
  1895 in Annapolis, MD, d: 29 Jun 1975
  married on 16 Feb 1925 in Annapolis, MD, to
Helen Elizabeth Lillian Litz (1896–unk) b: 07 Apr
  1896.
  They had four children.

Catherine Julia Musterman (1897–unk) b: 14 Sep 1897
married on 01 Jul 1918 to
Robert Jerome Zindorf
They had two children.

William Walter Musterman (1899–1899) b: 12 Oct
1899, d: 12 Oct 1899

Andrew Jesse Newton Musterman (1900–1960) b: 24
Dec 1900, d: 13 Aug 1960
married on 01 Nov 1919 to
Bertha Marguerite Lee (1902–1942) b: 10 Oct 1902,
d: 04 Feb 1942
They had three children.

James Walter Musterman (1903–1972) b: 24 Dec 1903,
d: 12 Jan 1972
married on 11 May 1927 to
Hilda Irene Lee (1907–unk) b: 07 Jan 1907
Unknown issue.

Andrew Hermann Musterman Jr. (1896–1896) b: 01
Aug 1896, d: 03 Sep 1896
married on 27 Oct 1886 to
Virginia Holliday
Unknown issue.

Unknown Musterman (–1887) d: 20 Feb 1887

John Henry Musterman (1859–1924) and Lillian Powell Johnson (1881–1980)

John Henry Musterman (1859–1924) b: 13 Aug 1859 in Annapolis, MD, d: 23 Dec 1924 at home in Annapolis, MD

married on 10 Sep 1908 at Nan (Lillian's sister) and Frank Parsons' home, Baltimore, MD, to

Lillian Powell Johnson (1881–1980) b: 08 Dec 1881 in Onancock, VA, d: 05 Apr 1980 in Bay Ridge Nursing Home, Annapolis, MD

They had three children:

John Henry Musterman III (1910–2003) b: 04 Feb 1910 in Annapolis, MD, d: 05 Jul 2003 in Baltimore, MD

married on 03 Oct 1934 to

Margaret Elizabeth Patterson (1911–2006) b: 04 Oct 1911, d: 08 May 2006 in Baltimore, MD

They had two children.

Powell Johnson Musterman (1910–1981) b: 04 Feb 1910 in Annapolis, MD,

married on 02 Jun 1936, d: 12 May 1981 in Annapolis, MD, to

Evelyn Lucille Harman (1912–1997) b: 11 Apr 1912 in Annapolis, MD, d: 01 Dec 1997 Annapolis, MD

They had two children.

Nancy Elizabeth Musterman (1916–2002) b: 20 May
1916 at home 9 Dean Street, Annapolis, MD, d: 10
Dec 2002 in Annapolis, MD
married on 05 Sept 1936 at 197 Main Street, Annapolis,
MD, to
James Thomas Reed (1912–1996) b: 28 Aug 1912 in
Trenton Jail, Trenton, TN, d: 26 Sep 1996 in Balti-
more, MD
They had three children.

Appendix B

THE METAMORPHOSIS
OF 197 MAIN STREET

I T FIRST WAS A Colonial-Era tavern and inn but just over one hundred years later a renovation turned 197 Main Street into a grand Victorian home. It remained that for twenty years, until it was partially renovated to create a hat shop. The milliner lived above her store for fifty-five years. Other stores followed; the apartments above became offices. Today (summer 2019) it is a sushi restaurant, and living quarters fill the upper levels again.

❧

The original structure at 197 Main Street (then Church Street) was built before the Revolution, about 1767. It was brick, English bond, and the center and larger of three attached structures: 195 (20 feet wide), 197 (28 feet wide), and 199 (unknown width). Each building had a left entrance, up a few steps from the street. The original buildings together are described as "a two-story, three-bay brick structure set on a raised stone foundation with a gable roof."[1] In 1767, the *Maryland Gazette* advertised the opening of a coffee house that is assumed to have been at the location of these buildings. While it is possible that the coffee house was originally at 197 Main Street and expanded into 195, these Georgian buildings were together known as the Coffee House until at least 1773. A notice appeared in the *Maryland Gazette* on May 12, 1780, advertising the buildings for lease and describing twenty-four rooms (four rooms on each floor), excluding garrets.

The Annapolis Coffee House was the site of many social and business meetings of the town and countryside elite, including the Lunatick Club and the Homony Club. George Washington mentions it often in his accounts of his visits to Annapolis, and Charles Carroll "waited on Patrick Henry [there] . . . who passed through on his way to Williamsburg."

By 1798, 195 Main Street was a "house of entertainment" and by 1806 it was leased as a "hair dressing shop" with residences above. The building at 195 Main Street was owned by one person in 1817, while the other two (197 and 199) had a different owner. About 1825, dormers were added to achieve a Federal look. Today, 195 Main Street retains some of its original eighteenth-century exterior and provides a hint of the look of the Colonial Era at the roof line. In the twentieth century, a stretcher bond façade was applied to the English bond walls on the front of 195 but the side wall still retains the original.[2]

The original structure at 199 Main Street was demolished between 1891 and 1893 and in its place an American Renaissance-style building was erected. It makes up three commercial units—199–201, 203–205, and 207 Main Street—that end at Ridout Alley. Each unit retains its nineteenth-century façade on the street storefront and residences above. The store at 205 was once a "hat cleaners and renovators" before becoming Julia Strange's millinery from 1908 to 1918.[3] In 1921 it was an optical shop, later Eckert's Jewelry Store, and today Ron George Jewelers. The book *The Years Between* provides a first-hand description of turn-of-the-century Annapolis and includes this account of the odd-numbered buildings below Ridout Alley to Conduit Street and above the alley to Church Circle in 1900:[4]

From this alley down Main Street to Conduit was a group of large brick homes with back yards extending through to Duke of Gloucester Street. There were the homes of Mr. Duvall [199], Dr. George Feldmeyer [197], Mr. George Moss [195], Dr. Frank Thompson, Dr. Joseph Worthington, then came a group of stores and the "Carroll-Davis" house on the corner. We remember when the Duval house gave way to the present row of stores on Main Street [formerly 199; now 199–207] and the row of houses in the back facing on Duke of Gloucester Street.

Those buildings above Ridout's Alley [*sic*] were the Great Emporium (owned by the Ridout brothers, Mr. Weems, and Mr. Grafton); George Feldmeyer's dental office [at 211] in a small frame building that once held the oldest firehouse, Old Pumper, in 1884; the Nichols home; the Chinese laundry, later a barbershop; and Maryland Hotel at Church Circle.[5]

When Dr. Feldmeyer bought the building at 197 Main

Street in 1897, it was a "tenement" and still had its Revolutionary-Era appearance.[6] Rather than retain the colonial façade, Dr. Feldmeyer had the structure entirely rebuilt to create the perfect turn-of-the-century home for his family, complete with indoor plumbing. They were in residence by the end of 1900.

He added two rooms at the back on the first and second floors and removed the original gabled roof to add a third story. He topped it off with a mansard roof with three dormers.[7]

The front of the building was replaced by a brick Italianate façade with a first-floor bay window that projected a couple feet over the sidewalk, drastically changing the look of this Main Street structure. The entry vestibule was on the left of the building, about four feet above the sidewalk on level with the first floor of the home. It appears a stairway built against the side of the house and parallel to the street led from the sidewalk to the outer vestibule door.[8, 9]

Today the original exterior vestibule door is gone, leaving visible from the sidewalk the marbleized tile enclosure, with a green-and-brown ivy motif above white. The style is typical of turn-of-the-century (nineteenth) tilework. In the vestibule to the left is a tiled alcove, perhaps for boots, coats, and umbrellas. Transoms installed above both exterior and interior doors remain, as does the interior double door that offered entry into the hallway of the house. Two carved wood panels comprise this double door, each with a single pane of glass.

Dr. Feldmeyer had the interior of the home renovated to match the latest trends. New floors, new stairways, and new hallways on each level. Fireplaces and gas lighting in all the rooms. The entrance hall had space for a large coat rack next to a broad stairway on the left. Wide hallways ran the length of each floor. Off the first-floor hallway, doorways to the front and back parlors and dining room were on the right. These rooms could be separated by pulling heavy pocket doors from the walls when desired. The door to the kitchen was at the end of the hall, just past a door on the left that opened to a stairwell to the basement. Behind a door in the kitchen was a staircase—for servants?—that was concealed and led to the upper two floors.

The second floor had six rooms and a large bathroom. Four rooms situated from the front to the back, with entry doorways from the hall and connecting doorways between them as well. A fifth room at the back had access from the fourth room only. The front room had two windows looking onto Main Street, and next to it, above the vestibule, was a small room that had one window onto Main Street and one to the side looking over the rooftops toward the city dock.

Both the open stairway from the entrance and the enclosed stairway at the back continued to the third floor. Perhaps maids called those rooms their home: a small room looking onto Main Street, a bedroom, and a bath at the back. When the George Feldmeyer family lived there, the maids would have climbed up and down the hidden staircases when doing the housekeeping.

The family used the open staircase and hallways along the left of the house. The interior throughout had dark-stained wood baseboards, wide wood door molding, and bull's-eye corner blocks in every door frame. Above each door was a glass transom to open for ventilation in the hot summers.

The home had three bathrooms—one on each floor. The

bathrooms on the first and third floors were at the back of the house and had one access door, but the second-floor bathroom was in the middle and had three doors: one from the hall, one from the front bedroom, and one from the second bedroom. It was the largest room on the second floor and spacious enough to hold several cabinets of linens and toiletries. Black and white tile covered the floor, a claw-footed tub sat under a window over the side alley. The commode was positioned far into a corner on a cement pedestal and faced the side of a marble sink with brass faucets.

Once the house was complete, the Feldmeyers moved in. Dr. Feldmeyer continued attending to his dental practice a few doors up Main Street in the office he maintained at 211 for years.[10]

Some years later, most likely Dr. Feldmeyer installed the radiators in front of all the fireplaces, disconnected the gas fixtures, and added the overhead electric lights in the center of every room, upstairs and down, complete with push-button controls by each door.

Before 1920, the Feldmeyers moved to yet another new home—this one at 2 Southgate Avenue, in the "suburbs." It was a short walk—about five blocks—to town and Dr. Feldmeyer's dental office. The house at 197 Main Street stood empty.

In June 1921, John Henry and Lillian Powell Musterman (née Johnson), a well-known milliner, bought the property for approximately $6,000. She had rented the building from George Feldmeyer for two years before he sold to her. He also held the mortgage.[11] She renovated the first-floor parlors for a shop but retained the dining room and kitchen on the first floor and all the rooms on the upper two floors as they were.[12]

Mrs. Musterman began at the front door to put her mark on the building. She demolished the entry stairway and removed the exterior door and floor to the vestibule. In their place she installed wooden stairs that rose at a right angle from the sidewalk through the vestibule space to the former interior double door. This became the front entrance to the house in 1921 and remains today.

To create her store from the two parlors, she walled them off, leaving no access or egress between store and house. She removed their fireplaces and floors as well as the bay window. She extended the storefront about three feet onto the sidewalk by breaking through and rebuilding the stone foundation. Once the demolition was complete, she installed a new floor that was at street level, and mounted a single large plate-glass window on a solid cement base. This storefront window with two smaller glass panels on the left and right enclosed a wide wooden sill—three feet deep. Passersby would see her hats displayed on the sill as well as those inside. Above the storefront were rectangular windows to let light stream in. To the right of the storefront was a new framed glass door entrance. Customers were sheltered from the elements by an overhang.

In the shop space, shelves were installed on the back and side walls, almost to the ceiling. A deep counter with wide drawers was placed to separate the selling area from the wrapping area and cash drawer. At the back right of the store and one step up, separated by a drawn curtain, was her workroom and small lavatory. When she was in business her two treadle sewing machines, one electric sewing machine, a steam kettle, hat blocks, and sewing threads filled the space. At the back of her work room was a window that opened onto the gap between the buildings and let in a bit of light from the yard and back alley.

In 1922, the Musterman family moved into the house and filled the first and second floors. Kitchen and dining room on the first. Sitting room and bedrooms on the second. The third floor became a one-bedroom apartment with sitting room, kitchen, and bath for tenants. The halls remained opened between the floors. Mrs. Musterman added two grand wrap-around porches onto the back of the house. The first-floor porch was entered from the kitchen and the hall on the left. The second-floor porch was accessed from the top of the stairs that led from the entrance hall of the house. Both porches were the full width of the house (twenty-eight feet) and were about sixteen feet deep.

In 1936, Mrs. Musterman converted the first-floor kitchen and dining room (on the common wall with the store) to a studio apartment where she lived until the mid-1950s. She created an apartment for her newly married son Powell and his family on the second floor by installing a kitchen in the small room above the vestibule. Those were the last changes made by Mrs. Musterman. The rest of the interior remained as when the Feldmeyer's had renovated it. Powell and his family lived in the second-floor apartment until the mid-1950s. At that time, Mrs. Musterman moved to the second floor and leased the first- and third-floor apartments.

This was 197 Main Street from 1921 until the 2000s. The store and the house had separate entrances but shared the same street address.

~

After Mrs. Musterman retired in 1967, she rented the store space first to a retail business called Kaleidoscope and next to the Charisma Shop. Other stores followed until the building was sold in 1976, when she moved to Annapolis Convalescent Center.[13] The owners that followed continued to lease the building to various retail businesses.

For thirteen years beginning in the early 1980s, Scottish and Irish Imports occupied the space.[14] Jim Hollan, owner of the business, removed the back wall of the store to extend the sales floor area to the back of the building, using the area of the former first-floor studio apartment. He installed a short stairway to reach this area. During the renovation, a colonial fireplace was uncovered in the location of the stove in the former kitchen. The old doors to the first-floor hallway, bathroom, and back stairs were visible to customers.

Beginning in the mid-1990s, Interior Concepts occupied the building. During their approximately ten-year tenancy, the now dilapidated grand porches on the second and third floors were removed. Interior Concepts decorators transformed the upstairs rooms to design studios. The Cook's Revenge, which sold culinary equipment and implements, was the last business in the space. When it vacated in late 2008, the Maryland Federation of Art mounted their Holiday Art Show in the space throughout December. And then the space was empty. During the years 1921 through 2008, Mrs. Musterman's renovations to 197 Main Street, inside and out, remained intact.

~

Next door, 195 Main Street was changing, too. Through the years, the upper floors were a residence to various families who entered from the original Colonial-Era, left-door entrance. But the downstairs continued to be commercial space. At some point a storefront window was added as was a door to the right of the building for entering the store. In the 1920s it was a barber shop; in the 1940s, "Your Hairdresser"; in the 1960s, a candy shop. After more iterations, 195 Main Street became the original location of the popular restaurant Café Normandie.

In 1993, the French restaurant moved down the street to a larger space, and a sushi restaurant—Joss Café and Sushi Bar—took its place. The operators, Joseph Shyue-Hae and Jane Yu-Chen Jiau, bought the property in 1995.[15]

In time, this restaurant also gained popularity, and the small space at 195 became untenable. By 2008 the owners of Joss had purchased the property next door, 197 Main Street. As renovations began, passersby could watch the demolition through the windows. Because of the building's location in the Annapolis Historic District, alterations by the architects were subject to review and approval by various entities such as the Annapolis Planning Commission and the citizen volunteer group Historic Preservation Commission (under the city's Department of Planning and Zoning's Historic Preservation Division). Historic Annapolis, Inc., may have been asked for guidance as well. Eventually, the owners of 195 Main Street successfully petitioned the city to expand their restaurant into 197 Main Street. They petitioned again to modify the approved expansion and applied for a liquor license.[16, 17]

The exterior of the building was not changed and remains

as it has been since 1921.[18] But a total interior demolition began. It stopped for a while and began again, perhaps because of the recession or requirements for archeology to be completed before renovations could resume.

The interior stairway went. The hallways went. The wall between 195 and 197 was broken through. The 1921 interior renovation was completely gutted. An interior wall extending from the left of the glass door to the store to the back of the store space was built to enclose a new staircase entered from the sidewalk. Up those stairs on the upper floors, walls came down and new walls went up. Kitchens and baths came out and new ones went in. And then, as the upstairs apartments were being completed, Joss Café and Sushi Bar opened its new dining room.

Access to Joss is through the glass-paned door at 195 Main Street. What was once a candy store now holds the host stand and service bar area. After being greeted, a customer follows the host up an inclined passageway. High on the right of the passageway, light streams in through the windows of the carved wood double door—the door that now leads to nowhere—the 1900 interior front door to the house at 197 Main Street. Continuing on, the customer arrives at the sushi bar or is seated at a table in the main dining room, both in the area of the former hat shop. The former store's plate-glass window remains, allowing sunshine to brighten the restaurant and passersby to view the diners.

The floors above the restaurant are now three apartments, accessed by a stairway entered by the former store's glass door. Through that door can be seen an exposed, framed area of colonial brick that appears to be a "relieving arch."[19]

The interiors of both 195 and 197 Main Street retain none of their original colonial features. At 195 Main Street the exterior side wall, constructed in the Colonial Era, retains its original English bond, and its gabled roof line is reminiscent of the period.

Aside from that bit of brickwork, nothing of the original colonial building of 197 Main Street survives. The nineteenth-century Italianate façade, mansard roof, tiled vestibule, and carved wooden interior double door remain from Dr. Feldmeyer's Victorian-period renovation to the eighteenth-century building. Of his Victorian interior, only one staircase remains: It leads from the second floor to the third-floor apartment.

Of Mrs. Musterman's renovations, the exterior recalls her changes to the building. The entrance stairs to the house, the large plate-glass window of the store, and the wood-framed glass door that was her store entrance remain.

Now again 195 and 197 Main Street share interior space as they did in colonial days to provide an eatery on the ground floor and with living quarters on the upper floors. One wonders when and how the metamorphosis will continue and what it will bring.

NOTES

1. At Mrs. Musterman's Hat Shop

1. Clarence Marbury White, Sr., and Evangeline Kaiser White, *The Years Between: A Chronicle of Annapolis, Maryland, 1800-1900 and Memoirs of,* New York: Exposition Press, Inc., 1957, p. 19.

2. Judy Klemesrud, "'Tea Fights' at Annapolis Introduces Plebes to Social Life." *New York Times.* May 6, 1969, p. 42. (https://www.nytimes.com/1969/05/06/archives/-tea-fight-at-annapolis-introduces-plebes-to-social-life.html). Tea dances at the Naval Academy where high school and college young women met midshipmen and they in turn practiced being gentlemen. But midshipmen first had to take dance lessons with other midshipmen. It's been said they fought over who would lead, thus the name tea fights.

3. A style of waving hair with metal crimps created in 1882 by Marcel Grateau and popular in the 1920s and 1930s.

4. Various personal communications, including Delores Addington, Janet Schrader Greentree, and Susan Crawford (a niece), via Facebook group Friends of Annapolis, April 2018.

2. Lil the Country Girl

1. Pronounced oh-nan-cock. A Native American name meaning foggy place. The town is up Onancock Creek from the Chesapeake Bay on the Eastern Shore of Virginia.

2. The history (mid 1600s to 1900) of the Tyler, Crockett, Hopkins, FitzGerald, and Johnson families in Onancock and on Tangier and Smith islands is available together with their complete genealogies and an index in *We Come From Island People* by Elizabeth Leah

Reed. Petersrow, 2006. (https://petersrow.com/catalog/catalog.
htm#A).

3. The building is listed on the Virginia Landmarks Register and the
   National Register of Historic Places. (https://www.shorehistory.
   org/hopkins-brothers).

4. *Peninsula Enterprise,* June 8, 1882.

5. Kathryn Lilliston, niece of Lillian Powell Musterman. Personal
   communication, 1990s.

6. Mame Warren and Marion E. Warren, *Maryland Time Expo-
   sures:1840–1940*, Baltimore, MD: Time Exposures Limited, 1984,
   p. 169.

7. Bugeyes and pungies were built similarly to the early log canoes
   but with more logs. Precursors of the skipjack, these narrow wood-
   en vessels were more than 50 ft from stem-to-stern, with a 15-ft
   beam. The rounded log bottom of the bugeye had a shoal draft of
   2 to 3 ft with the centerboard up—ideal for harvesting oysters in
   the shallow waters of the Chesapeake Bay. The masts carried huge
   sails and a jib. The sail area was about 1,700 sq ft, ensuring swift
   movement over the waters of the Bay. A low aft cabin provided a
   place to sleep.

8. The late Kathryn Johnson Lilliston, Margaret Johnson Elmore,
   and Lillian Hayman Sweigart, nieces of Lillian P. Musterman.
   Various personal communications, 1990s.

9. The widowed Margaret Hopkins Johnson raised her family at 10
   Holly Street (no longer standing) built by her father-in-law (Thomas Johnson, Cap'n Tom) next to his farmhouse at 9 Holly.

10. Mary Felter, personal communication, taped interview with Lillian
    P. Musterman, Annapolis Convalescent Center, February 10, 1978.

11. Ibid.

12. Eleanor Owings, "Musty, This Is Your Life," Script for Zonta's

Ninetieth Birthday Celebration for Lillian P. Musterman. December 1971, unpublished.

13. The house is often on the spring house tour.

14. This home is now known as the Alicia Hopkins house. One of the oldest structures in Onancock, it is often featured on the annual spring house tour.

15. Anne Nock, current owner the Alicia Hopkins house, personal communication, abt. 2006.

16. The house was provided by her father Stephen Hopkins when she was widowed early in the Civil War.

17. Felter, Interview.

18. Elizabeth Leah Reed, "Appomattox to Alturas: Correspondence of Nehemiah FitzGerald, First County Clerk of Modoc County, As Revealed Through His Letters," *Modoc County Historical Society,* No. 40, 2018, p. 119–196. Also appears as Appendix B: Letters, *We Come From Island People,* Petersrow, 2006, also by Elizabeth Leah Reed.

19. Pronounced *car.* Today the Ker Place Museum is operated by the Eastern Shore of Virginia Historical Society. It is open to the public. (https://www.shorehistory.org/ker-place).

20. Lillian P. Musterman, personal communication, Letter to Catherine "Kitty" Hayman Jackson from Annapolis, MD, April 22, 1969.

21. Note: The tree was cut down in 1991.

22. Felter, Interview.

23. Ibid.

24. Ibid.

25. Musterman, personal communication, Letter.

3. Young Lil Becomes a Milliner

1. From the seventeenth-century English term "millianer," which described those who fashioned feminine caps and bonnets after the style of "Millayne bonnets" being made in the Duchy of Milan.

2. The firm was almost 100 years old in 1900. Descriptions here are from "Armstrong, Cator & Company: 1805–1910," *The Illustrated Milliner*, January 1910. The original building was completely destroyed in the Great Baltimore Fire of 1904.

3. Olive Ann Burns, *Cold Sassy Tree*, New York: Hougton Mifflin Company, 2007, p. 24.

4. Angela Serratore, "Keeping Feathers Off Hats—And On Birds," Smithsonianmag.com, May 15, 2018. Feathers were most desired from the late 1800s to the early 1900s. So much so that the Migratory Bird Act was passed in 1918 to protect a vanishing avian population. In one year alone (1902) more than a ton of egret feathers were sold. Along with the millinery industry, collectors, hunters, and scientist contributed equally. Women in feathered hats were called the "indifferent followers of fashion." After passage of the act, feathered hats were created with dyed chicken and ostrich feathers.

5. Ibid.

6. Owings, "Musty, This Is Your Life," Zonta script.

7. This is how Mrs. Musterman always said it—*millincies*—vocabulary now gone, together with the days of the grand millinery houses.

8. Buckram is a stiff-finished, heavily sized fabric, usually linen or cotton. It is still used for millinery frames today, as then. The stiffening comes from using glue as the sizing that fills the gaps in the weave.

4. Lillian Arrives in Annapolis

1. "The Present Annapolis: The Venice on the Chesapeake," April 21, 1896, publisher unknown, photograph in Marion E. Warren and Mame Warren, *The Train's Done Gone: An Annapolis Portrait, 1889–1910*. Annapolis, MD: Marion E. Warren. 1976, p. 63. "The Venice on the Chesapeake" is also mentioned in Robin R. Cutler, *A Soul on Trial: A Marine Corps Mystery at the Turn of the Twentieth Century*, 2007 p. 45. But in the nineteenth century, Annapolis was known as the "Athens of America," the name given by Supreme Court Chief Justice Roger Brook Taney as noted by Ralph Crosby in *Memoirs of a Main Street Boy*. Anaphora Literary Press. 2016, p. 28.

2. The author has vivid memories of her train rides across that bridge.

3. Staff and Volunteers of Historic Annapolis, Inc., "Fact Sheets for Interpreters on Preservation, Restoration and History of Annapolis," 1967, unpublished. Also "Maryland Inventory of Historic Properties, Property AA-658 Feldmeyer-Gassaway House" [194 Prince George Street] Maryland Historical Trust. (https://bit.ly/3kcvDDC).

4. Marjorie (later Maples) and Dorothy (later Mrs. Edwin I. McQuinston), both of whom married Naval Academy graduates. Janie was the last of the Feldmeyer line to live in the large three-story house. (White and White, *The Years Between*, p. 124.). She became a lifelong friend of Lillian's.

5. James D. Feldmeyer owned the house from 1903 and was living there in 1910 with his father, sisters, and nieces. He might have lived there in 1900, as well. Frances Jaques, "Home of the Week: 'Victorian Style: House sparkling example of period,'" *The Capital*. October 10, 1987.

6. According to "Maryland Inventory of Historic Properties,

Property AA-1324, 203-205 Main Street," (Maryland Historical Trust), it was a "hat cleaners and renovators" before becoming Julia Strange's millinery. Once Eckert's Jewelry Store (1970s), today it is Ron George Jewelry.(https://bit.ly/36rrEOR).

7. White & White, *The Years Between*, p. 117. Also Warren & Warren, *Maryland Time Exposures*, p. 174.

8. Warren & Warren, *The Train's Done Gone*, p. 63.

9. Maryland's state house is the oldest state capitol building still in use today.

10. Felter, interview.

11. An online inflation calculator estimates $60 in 1905 at approximately $200 in 1960 dollars. (https://bit.ly/3eLgPuq).

12. Robert J. Brugger, *Maryland: A Middle Temperament, 1634–1980*, The Johns Hopkins Press, Baltimore, MD, 1988, p. 436.

13. Mame Warren and Marion Warren, *Everybody Works But John Paul Jones: A Portrait of the U.S. Naval Academy, 1845–1915*, Annapolis, MD: Naval Institute Press, 1981, pp. 48–49 and pp. 90–91.

14. Millineries as they appear in the city directory: Annapolitan Millinery Co., 55 Maryland ave.; Dawes, W. A., Mrs., 147 Main st.; Hardisty, Ijams, Miss, 142 Main st.; Holidayoke, M. F., Mrs., 172 Main st.; Strange, J. M., Mrs., 205 Main st.; Woolley, F. M., Miss, 2 West st., *Annapolis City Directory*, 1910, p. 136.

15. The 1859 structure of Calvary Methodist Church had a center pulpit to signify that the Bible is the foundation of the faith rather than the sacraments, a style common in many Protestant churches until the late nineteenth century. The building was razed in the 1970s to make way for state government office buildings, and the congregation moved to a new structure on Rowe Boulevard. Wesley Chapel later became the home of the Christian Science Church.

16. Dr. George Feldmeyer lived at 197 Main Street. Two early Annapolis city directories (1910 and 1924), list his dental office at 211 Main Street. White & White, *The Years Between*, p. 17, note that Feldmeyer's office was in a frame building that was "formerly a pumper station, and once the oldest firehouse in Annapolis" next to the Chinese laundry at the top of Main Street.

17. John Henry Musterman was once a part owner of Gilbert's with John Feldmeyer. The State Comptroller records note many payments to Gilbert and Musterman, pharmacy, for minor items from 1898 through 1906. About the turn of the century, other records indicate that the legislature considered banning non-pharmacists from owning a pharmacy. Perhaps John Musterman left the partnership at that time.

5. Miss Johnson Becomes Mrs. Musterman

1. Owings, "Musty, This Is Your Life," Zonta script.

2. Brugger, *Maryland*, p. 433.

3. Ibid. p. 434.

4. The witnesses signed the wedding guest book as follows: J. Kos. Parker, Helen R. Hoge, W. Hoge, Bernard Julian Hoge, Kate Tindall Samuels, Edwin F. Samuels, Dr. Wm. H. Feddeman, Virginia M. Feddeman, Emma D. Feddeman, Bessie L. Wightman, Alice Wightman, Donnell Parker, Nannie Parsons, Frank T. Parsons, Julia M. Strange, Elisabeth Hein, and Rev. Harry D. Mitchell, M.E, Clergyman. Dr. Feddeman was Lillian's cousin, his mother was a Johnson and the family was from Onancock. Dr. Feddeman had operated on Margaret Johnson, Lillian's mother, shortly before her death in 1902. It is unclear for what, but may have been for some type of cancer.

5. *Peninsula Enterprise*, September 10, 1908.

6. The Mustermans of Dean Street

1. John Henry Musterman's brother Andrew Henry Musterman named his son John Henry Musterman II after their father fifteen years before John and Lillian's sons were born; therefore, John and Lillian appended the numeral III to their son John Henry's name. See Appendix A: Who Were Those Mustermans, for details about this family since the first John Henry (unnumbered)—Johann Heinrich Mustermann—arrived in the United States in 1853. See Appendix A also for the Musterman genealogy.

2. At that time, women usually stayed in bed and in privacy for between two weeks and two months during the postpartum confinement period to recuperate from childbirth.

3. Nancy Musterman Reed, personal papers, unpublished.

4. The notorious public hanging happened in Annapolis on February 28, 1919, when the boys were nine and Nancy was three. Two key witnesses recanted their testimony, and eleven of the twelve jurors wanted Snowden's sentence commuted. Today there is no doubt about the grave miscarriage of justice dealt to an innocent man when John Snowden was convicted and hanged. He was pardoned by Maryland Gov. Glendening in 2001. (Jay Apperson and Andrea F. Siegel, "Glendening Pardons Black in 1919 Murder." *The Baltimore Sun*, June 1, 2001. (https://bit.ly/3lkzEaj) also "In Annapolis: Reconciled by a Pardon." *Bay Weekly*, vol 9 No 26 June 28–July 4, 2001. (https://bit.ly/2JYRbaB).

5. Kitty Burdette, "The Magnificent Milliner," *The Annapolitan*, April 1978.

6. Nan and Frank Parsons lived at 909 East Capitol Street. Washington, DC. It was their son, Frank, Jr., who founded Frank Parsons' Paper Company in Washington in 1938 with one truck, a storefront, and three employees. The business became a division of The Supply Rooms Companies (TSRC), Inc. in 2011.

7. Her former husband, Mayor James French Strange, served the city of Annapolis from 1909 to 1919. *Maryland Archives online MSA SC 3520-12685*. Also, J.F. Strange was "... four times elected mayor of Annapolis and also served as state Senator." White & White, *The Years Between*. p. 122.

8. According to "MIHP: Property AA-1324 203–205 Main Street," the store at 205 was Julia Strange's millinery from 1908 to 1913. The 1913 is assumed to be a typographical error, given the next footnote. Previously it was a "hat cleaners and renovators." The building was "vacant" in 1924, according to the *Annapolis City Directory*.

9. "Wanted" Young lady ... ," *Evening Capital*, September 9, 1918.

10. "Stylish Display of Fall Millinery," describes the new hats of Miss F. M. Wooley and Mrs. J. M. Strange. *Evening Capital*, October 1, 1918, p. 1.

11. William Oliver Stevens, *Annapolis: Anne Arundel's Town*, New York: Dodd, Mead & Company, 1937, p. 324.

12. "More Flu Cases: Victims Increase," *Evening Capital*, October 2, 1918, p. 1.

13. Thomas O. Tilghman, Sr., moved from the Eastern Shore to Annapolis 1898 and worked for Caldwell Jewelers on Maryland Avenue from 1928 until, in the 1940s, he established his fine jewelry store on State Circle.

14. Owings, "Musty, This Is Your Life," Zonta script.

15. Felter, Interview. It is not known if Mrs. Tilghman and Mrs. Strange's sister were the same person.

7. A Shop of Her Own

1. Felter, Interview.

2. More detail about these buildings, then and now, is provided in Appendix C: The Metamorphosis of 197 Main Street.

3. White & White, *The Years Between,* p. 17. Also Dr. Feldmeyer's office is listed in both the 1910 and 1924 Annapolis City phone directories as being at 211 Main Street.

4. It was deeded from George T. Feldmeyer to John and Lillian Musterman Liber WNW 42 Folio 305 as listed in "Maryland Inventory of Historic Properties, AA-576, 197 Main Street," Maryland Historic Trust (https://bit.ly/2IdTOor) .

5. After the renovation, the building had an entrance to the store and a separate entrance to the house, with no access from one to the other. Both shared the address 197 Main Street. For more details on the renovation, see Appendix C: The Metamorphosis of 197 Main Street.

8. The Key to Her Success

1. Felter, Interview.

2. Shirley Kimi Kim-Ng (née Wilsman), personal communication, via Facebook Messenger, May 17, 2018. (The bride was her sister Ethel Wilsman Bilderback.)

3. Kimbo, Ethelda "Peggy," personal communication, June 2010. Miss Peggy also told this story to the late Ginger Doyel who recounted it in her column "Annapolis From Past to Present" as "Life in the 1930s on College Avenue," *The Capital,* October 15, 2003, p. 15. It also appeared in *Annapolis Vignettes,* Tidewater Press, 2005, by Ms. Doyel.

4. Burdett, "The Magnificent Milliner."

5. Laura Sisson Downie, personal communication via Facebook Friends of Annapolis group, June 2016.

6. Roscoe C. Rowe, III, personal communication, via Facebook

Friends of Annapolis group, May 2018. His grandmother was Regina Rowe, the widow of former mayor Roscoe C. Rowe for whom Rowe Blvd. is named.

7. Owings, "Musty, This Is Your Life," Zonta script.

8. Advertisement. *Evening Capital,* July 11, 1887, p. 3.

9. "Newest Fashions In Winter Hats: Autumn Millinery Opening at the Holidayoke Company Today," *Evening Capital*, September 25, 1918, p 1.

10. "Millinery Opening," *Evening Capital*, September 28, 1918, p. 4.

11. "Stylish Display of Fall Millinery," *Evening Capital,* October 1, 1918, p. 1.

12. Maryland State Archives, photograph MSA SC 2140-689.

13. "Beautiful Doll in Display Window of Musterman Shop," *Evening Capital,* October 3, 1929.

14. The group was Army-Navy class of 42–43 Officer's Wives as noted in "Blooms and Straws Blossom into Gay Hats," *Evening Capital,* May 4, 1950, p. 5.

15. Anne Pidkowicz, personal communication, April 24, 2020.

16. Sharie Valereo, personal communication via Facebook Friends of Annapolis group, June 2016.

17. "History of Hats," (with many illustrations of hats through the centuries) (https://bit.ly/3kiboo7); "Women's Hat History, Hatworks. (https://bit.ly/3klms3N); and "History of Hats—All That's Interesting" (https://bit.ly/35j33wa).

18. Emily Post, *Etiquette: the Blue Book of Social Usage*, Ninth Edition, Funk & Wagnalls Company, New York, 1958.

9. Life Above the Store

1. Crosby, *Memoirs of a Main Street Boy*, p. 28.

2. Other tenants through the years included John's niece Emma Westphal Fordyce and her husband Emmett, John and Nancy Cragen, John and Mary O'Connell, and nephews Wayne Westphal and Conrad Gaw. Reed, personal papers.

3. Today an even newer bridge called the Naval Academy Bridge spans the river. Like the old drawbridge, it is designated part of MD 450 and leads to MD 2 (Ritchie Highway). A second Severn River bridge, now known as Pearl Harbor Memorial Bridge, was built in the 1950s a few miles upriver when John Hanson Highway (US 50) was built as the gateway road that leads to the Chesapeake Bay Bridge.

4. Ruby Young Miller, photograph caption in "Recollections—Part II," *Anne Arundel County History Notes*, Vol. XXVIII, No. 4, July 1997, p. 1.

10. The Years Between: 1924–1956

1. Lillian Musterman bought five plots at Cedar Park Cemetery and ordered a large headstone carved simply with the word MUSTER-MAN. It is on the main road inside the property. A granddaughter plans on using one of the remaining plots.

2. Nan's millinery was on Pennsylvania Avenue in Washington, DC. Reed, Personal papers.

3. Owings, "Musty, This Is Your Life," Zonta script.

4. Thurston's show was more than just magic. It was similar to the Ziegfeld Follies and toured the country just as the Ringling Circus did. He is considered to have been one of America's greatest magicians from 1908 until 1936.

5. When Zonta celebrated its 50th anniversary in June 1979, of the sixteen charter members, Mrs. Musterman was the only one still living. She was 97. "Local Zonta Club celebrates 50th year." *Evening Capital,* June 19, 1979, p. 6.

6. Dates are provided in the genealogy in Appendix A.

7. John's daughters, Peggy and Joanie; Powell's two, Sallie and Jay; Nancy's three: Nancy, Elizabeth, and Jim.

8. "Guest of Mrs. Musterman," *Evening Capital,* June 28, 1944, p. 5.

9. City-wide celebration of the 300th anniversary of the founding of Annapolis.

10. Mame Warren (quoting Jane Wilson McWilliams), *Then Again . . . Annapolis, 1900–1965,* Annapolis, MD: Time Exposures Limited, 1990, p. 144.

11. Arlington, Virginia (three times); Newport, Rhode Island; Philadelphia, Pennsylvania (twice); Charleston, South Carolina; London, England; Long Beach, California; and retirement in Memphis, Tennessee.

12. "Fourteen Gather for Musterman Reunion," *Evening Capital,* July 17, 1953, p. 5.

13. "Hurricane Hazel Rips Through Annapolis," *Evening Capital,* October 16, 1954, p. 1.

14. Historic Annapolis, Inc., was beginning to have influence in Annapolis as it strived to protect historically significant structures to create a "living colonial town." Fortunately it has had great success.

15. And today, more than fifty years later, *her* storefront is required not to be changed.

16. "City Firemen Quench Oil Burner Flare-Up," *Evening Capital,* October 11, 1956, p. 1.

11. Fire!

1. "15 Routed As Fire Damages Main Street Shops," *Evening Capital*, April 24, 1957, p. 1.

2. Cynthia Collins, personal communication via Facebook group "Friends of Annapolis," April 2018.

3. Mrs. Philip Sierliny, Mr. and Mrs. L. Thomas Whittington, Mrs. William A. Suchin, and Mrs. Lottie L. Lockwood.

4. Owings, "Musty, This Is Your Life," Zonta script.

5. "Letters to the Editor, 'Thank you,'" *Evening Capital*, May 4, 1957.

6. L.P. Musterman advertisement. *Evening Capital*, May 13, 1957.

7. "Busiest Day In Its 38 Years Marks Hatshop's [*sic*] Reopening," *Evening Capital*, August 15, 1957, p. 9.

8. Ibid.

9. "Shady Side News," *Evening Capital*, Thursday August 21, 1957, p. 6.

10. "Busiest Day," *Evening Capital*, p. 9.

12. Last Waltz

1. Since the 1978, Hats in the Belfry, at the foot of Main Street, has sold hats exclusively.

2. Jane Wilson McWilliams, *Annapolis, City on the Severn: A History*, Baltimore, MD: The Johns Hopkins University Press. Crownsville, MD: The Maryland Historical Trust Press, June 2011, p. 334.

3. Years later, in November 1990, Beth Whaley brought Mrs. Musterman back to life on the stage of St. John's College in the play "The Annapolis I Remember," directed by Sharie Lacey Valerio. It and the book *Then Again … Annapolis, 1900–1965* by Mame Warren

were the culmination of The Annapolis I Remember project to collect oral histories and photographs from 1900 to 1965.

4. "L.P. Musterman Hat Shop," photograph no. 84, *Annapolis Faces*, Annapolis Festival Foundation, Inc., no copyright, undated.

5. "L.P. Musterman Shop Is First One Finished," *Evening Capital*, October 18, 1961, p. 1.

6. Sigrid Theobald, "Letters to the Editor, 'Mrs. Musterman's Gift,'" *Evening Capital*, June 29, 1967, p. 4.

7. They bought 195 Main Street in 1995 ("MIHP Property AA-574 195 Main Street") and 197 Main Street sometime later.

8. See Appendix B: Metamorphosis of 197 Main Street, for a detailed account of these changes.

9. Attendees list from Owings, "Musty, This Is Your Life," Zonta script and "Zonta Member Honored," *Evening Capital*, December 16, 1971. Twin sons and wives: John and Helen Musterman, Powell and Lou Musterman. Daughter and husband: Nancy and Tom Reed. Grandchildren: Elizabeth Leah Reed (then Miller) and Jay Musterman. Other relatives: Niece Ruby Westphal Chaney and her son Jack as well as grandniece Dorothy Westphal Beatty (née Hall). Friends: Mrs. Edwin I. McQuiston, daughter of Mrs. Brewer (one of the Feldmeyer sisters) with whom she boarded at the Feldmeyer House; Mrs. Alfred Jefferson who was living at 1 Dean Street and had in 1910. Former assistant Pearl Zang. Millinery salesman Mr. Eric Lowenthal of Baltimore. Zontians: Mrs. Frederick C. Margraff, president of the club; Dorothy Dye, chairman of the program committee; Laura Armbruster, former president; Jeannette Joachim; Elizabeth Munroe; and Eleanor Owings—presenter of program.

10. Children of a marriage of one's granddaughter and the other's grandson.

11. Photo "Mrs. Musterman, Mother's Day Queen" *Evening Capital,* May 18, 1977, p. 28.

12. "Death Notices: 'Musterman on April 5, 1980, Lillian P,'" *Evening Capital,* April 7, 1980, p. 20.

13. Felter, Interview.

Appendix A: Who Were Those Mustermans?

1. A German will chuckle if the name *Mustermann* is mentioned, as happened to a great-grandson of Mrs. Musterman. That name is used in Germany as a place holder, similar to *John Doe* in the United States. During the 1970s, the name Max Mustermann appeared in German ads and on forms when new identification cards and passports were being introduced. Sometimes when *Mustermann* is entered into a German-to-English translator, *Doe* is the English result. *Muster* means template or pattern in German.

2. No departure passenger lists are available for those emigrants sailing from Bremen to Baltimore. "Due to limited space and to the idea that the emigrants would be lost for their German native country, the Bremen passenger lists were destroyed in 1875." *Passenger Departure Lists of German Emigrants, 1709–1914* by Friedrich R. Wollmershäuser, 1997. (web page no long available). Perhaps that explains the gap between 1834 and 1855 in a "complete list of sailings from Bremen to Baltimore" found online. Johann Heinrich Mustermann would have arrived in Baltimore during that gap.

3. Warren & Warren, *Maryland Time Exposures,* pp. 127–129.

4. Baltimore Immigration Museum (https://bit.ly/3nbd0Sl), free link to family search.org/Baltimore (visited October 2016).

5. Gisela Mustermann-Fiedler of Gehrde, Germany, personal communication via email, October 2016. "Neuenkirchen is a village 12 km near Gehrde."

6. After much research on various genealogy websites based in both the United States and Germany, as well as Gisela Mustermann-Fiedler's personal genealogy records, no Johann Heinrich Mustermann was located with his known birth date within any Mustermann line in Germany. Did they just forget him when he emigrated?

7. Gehrde is a Gemeinde (parish) in Bersenbrück Samtgemeinde (consolidated parish), which is in Osnabrück district/county (Landkreis). When called "*the* Gehrde," the reference is to Gehrde Gegend—the Gehrde area/land. The Dorf Gehrde is the village and earlier a castle or fortress in feudal days.

8. Johann Mustermann was clearly German, but various U.S. censuses and editions of *Annapolis, Maryland, Families* confuse his origins. In some instances he is recorded correctly as being born in Germany and others incorrectly with Holland as his birthplace. His granddaughter Nancy Musterman Reed believed that her grandparents never learned English. Perhaps when asked "place of birth" he responded *Deutsch* meaning Germany, but the census taker heard "Dutch" and erroneously recorded Holland. He sometimes is also recorded as coming from Marburg, Germany, where there are many Mustermanns, but that is also in error.

9. *Matchett's Baltimore Directory* for 1853–1854, Vol. 0564, p. 0224.

10. White & White, *The Years Between*, p. 123–124. Also, Maryland Inventory of Historic Properties, Property AA-658 Feldmeyer-Gassaway House" [194 Prince George Street]. Maryland Historic Trust. (https://bit.ly/3kgeZTK).

11. By 1903, the home belonged to James Feldmeyer, one of Gottlieb's eleven children and one-time business partner of John Musterman, Johann's son. Jacques, "Victorian Style." Another Feldmeyer property was a farm across Spa Creek from Annapolis in Eastport on Burnside Street. Huge family gatherings such as the annual Fourth of July picnic included the Mustermans.

12. Passenger Information 1820–1872, Catharina Rehn AR 31 Aug 1837 Altenmuhr, G F Bremen, *Gustav*, age 38 National Archives M255, Microfile roll 2, List No. 55. Annie was ten. Is this her mother?

13. Nancy Musterman Reed, personal communication. In the 1950s, Nancy visited Marburg (then in the postwar French sector), mistakenly thinking her grandfather had come from there. She had an "American Express" moment when she found the town's phone directory was filled with Mustermanns.

14. McWilliams, *Annapolis*, p. 234, and "Family discovers special edition of *Evening Capital* from more than 100 years ago," *The Capital*, April 1, 2016. Describes the Special Edition of the *Evening Capital*, "Historical and Industrial Edition: Portraying the Glorious Past and Future Possibilities of Annapolis, Maryland," May 1908, *Evening Capital*.

15. *Annapolis City Directory: 1910.* (https://bit.ly/36tvRBy).

16. McWilliams, *Annapolis*, p. 204.

17. Ibid, p. 269.

18. "MIHP, Property AA-32 Baron deKalb Monument." (https://bit.ly/32rUdKL)

19. McWilliams, *Annapolis*, p. 204.

20. Born in Altona, a suburb of Hamburg, Germany, John William Henry Westphal had left Germany on a merchant vessel in 1857, immigrated and worked as a painter in Baltimore from 1862 to 1867, then enlisted in the U.S. Navy at Annapolis, MD, for three years as "Thomas Beech."

21. John and Lillian Musterman had lived there from 1910 until 1922. Their three children—the twins John and Powell and their daughter Nancy—were born in that house.

22. *Annapolis City Directory: 1924.*

23. Ibid.

24. Robert Harry McIntyre, *Annapolis, Maryland, Families,* Baltimore, MD: Gateway Press. 1979.

25. A genealogist would number the John Henry Mustermans as I for Johann; II his son John Henry, and III for *his* son John (b. 1910). But that's not how the family did it. The son of Andrew (nephew of John Henry) was John Henry II, and John Henry's son John Henry (b. 1910) was always John Henry III.

26. *Annapolis City Directory: 1924* lists Bertha Lee (Andrew Jesse Musterman's wife) as Margt—short for her middle name Marguerite.

27. "Renewal Ideas Sought for West Street Buildings," *The Capital,* December 27, 2000, p. 37.

28. Amy Oakes, "Council Approves Mayor's Budget, 2001," *The Baltimore Sun*, May 23, 2000. (https://bit.ly/36iJZxk).

29. Donna Ware, personal communication. With city budget approval, including funds for the Knighton Garage on West Street, the Mayor created the Knighton Property Development Program Objectives Committee. Its charge was to guide the design process and report by June 15, 2000. The eleven-member committee recommended that the buildings be saved and incorporated into the overall design as a buffer for the garage complex. Ms. Ware was a member of the committee and is the former executive director of Historic London Town & Gardens, September 2019.

30. Ellen Moyer, personal communication, October 11, 2020.

31. "Knighton, Cecil Claggett," *The Baltimore Sun*, July 14, 2007. (https://bit.ly/38tQrEo).

32. This row of buildings was last visited by the author in 2017.

33. The author maintains the complete genealogy through six generations and is indebted to the late Raymond Disney and Dorothy Beatty (née Hall) for generously sharing their genealogy information. They both provided the family tree created by Andrew Jesse

Musterman and added to it from their own knowledge of the Musterman descendants. Other sources include *Annapolis, Maryland, Families,* Ancestry.com, and various German genealogy websites. A personal contact with Gisela Mustermann-Fiedler of Gehrde, Germany, yielded her detailed genealogy, but no Johann Heinrich. No information thus far investigated relates the Annapolis Musterman family to any records of Mustermans "over the pond." The author made careful choices from many conflicting dates and spellings; therefore, disagreement may exist.

Appendix B: The Metamorphosis of 197 Main Street

1. "MIHP Property AA-574 195 Main Street," "MIHP Property AA-576 197 Main Street," and "MIHP Property AA-1324 203-205 Main Street."

2. Ibid.

3. It appears that "MIHP Property AA-1324 203-205 Main Street" is incorrect in stating that the store at 205, Julia Strange's millinery, existed from 1908 to 1913. The 1913 is assumed to be a typographical error, because an advertisement appeared in the *Evening Capital* on September 9, 1918, noting that Mrs. Strange's millinery needed a young lady. The building was "vacant" in 1924 according to the *Annapolis City Directory: 1924.*

4. White & White, *The Years Between,* p. 19.

5. Ibid, p. 16–19.

6. Jeremiah Hughes Gray, wife et al. to George T. Feldmeyer, Liber GW 9, Folio 264, 1898 as listed in "MIHP Property AA-576 197 Main Street."

7. Popular in the late 1800s, a mansard roof is a four-sided gambrel-style hip roof characterized by two slopes on each side. Dormer windows puncture the lower slope. It creates an additional

floor of habitable space (a garret), thus reducing the overall height of the roof. (https://bit.ly/3pd0FyW).

8. The position of the original eighteenth-century door was also to the left.

9. Sanborn Fire Insurance Map from Annapolis, Anne Arundel County, Maryland. Sanborn Map Company, Oct. 1908. Map. (https://bit.ly/2Ito4uU).

10. Dr. Feldmeyer's dentistry office was probably never in his home at 197 Main Street, as stated in the summary of "MIHP Property AA-576 197 Main Street" for this building. His office is listed in both the 1910 and 1924 Annapolis phone directories as being at 211 Main Street. That location is also given by White & White, *The Years Between*, p. 16. And, according to "Maryland Inventory of Historic Properties, Property AA-581 [211 Main Street]. Maryland Historic Trust. (https://bit.ly/2GNNtjJ), George Feldmeyer bought 211 Main Street from the Inglehart family in 1912. By 1921, the building was converted into a grocery store. Following George Feldmeyer's death, John Roger Fredland purchased the property in 1960.

11. "MIHP Property AA-576 197 Main Street." George T. Feldmeyer to John and Lillian Musterman, Liber WNW 42 Folio 305, 1921.

12. The renovation described here is from first-hand accounts of Mrs. Musterman to the author and other family members and not contained in "MIHP Property AA-576 197 Main Street." That source briefly refers to its having been called a store, notes some changes, and describes the building at a time when Interior Concepts was the tenant, about 2000.

13. "MIHP Property AA-576 197 Main Street." Lillian P. Musterman, widow, to Nelson R. Knox, Liber 2900 Folio 124, 1976.

14. Jim Hollan incorporated Scottish and Irish Imports in December 1982 (https://bit.ly/3po9wy3). It operated for thirteen years (prweb.com/releases/2008/08/prbeb1212884.htm) and Michael R.

Driscoll, "Writer Reaches Back To His Mail Order Days," *The Baltimore Sun*, Jan. 3, 1991 (https://bit.ly/3kjt8Q2).

15. "MIHP AA-574 Property 195 Main Street." 195 Main Street Association to Joseph Shyue-Hae and Jane Yu-Chen Jiau, Liber 6294 Folio 645, 1995.

16. "Notice of Meeting, 'Public Hearing and Deliberation, 1.'" *The Capital*, September 8, 2010, p. 29.

17. "Notice of Hearing," *The Capital*, October 25, 2010, p. 23.

18. Donna Ware, personal communication. August 2010. While the streetscapes can be changed with approval, generally historic district streetscapes remain as they were in the 1970s when Historic Annapolis Foundation prepared drawings to encourage streetscape and building façade preservation.

19. Ibid. The brick arch appears to have been filled or may have been originally filled and may have been a "relieving arch," an architectural technique to add extra strength to the load-bearing wall.

WORKS CITED

"15 Routed As Fire Damages Main Street Shops." *Evening Capital.* April 24, 1957.

Annapolis City Directory: 1910. (http://msa.maryland.gov/megafile/ msa/speccol/sc2900/sc2908/000001/000542/html/am542-- 123.html).

Annapolis City Directory: 1924. (http://msa.maryland.gov/megafile/ msa/speccol/sc2900/sc2908/000001/000538/html/am538--23. html).

Annapolis Faces. Annapolis Festival Foundation, Inc., not copyrighted, undated (c 1965).

Apperson, Jay, and Andrea F. Siegel. "Glendening Pardons Black in 1919 Murder." *The Baltimore Sun.* June 1, 2001. (https://www. baltimoresun.com/news/bs-xpm-2001-06-01-0106010310-story. html).

"Armstrong, Cator & Company: 1805–1910." *The Illustrated Milliner.* January 1910.

Baltimore Immigration Museum has link to familysearch.org/Balti- more. (http://www.immigrationbaltimore.org/).

"Beautiful Doll in Display Window of Musterman Shop." *Evening Capital.* October 3, 1929.

"Blooms and Straws Blossom into Gay Hats." *Evening Capital.* May 4, 1950.

Brugger, Robert J. *Maryland: A Middle Temperament, 1634–1980*. Baltimore, MD: The Johns Hopkins University Press, 1988.

Burdette, Kitty. "The Magnificent Milliner." *The Annapolitan*. April 1978.

Burns, Olive Ann. *Cold Sassy Tree*. New York: Hougton Mifflin Company. 2007.

"Busiest Day In Its 38 Years Marks Hatshop's [sic] Reopening." *Evening Capital*. August 15, 1957.

"City Firemen Quench Oil Burner Flare-Up." *Evening Capital*. October 11, 1956.

Crosby, Ralph. *Memoirs of a Main Street Boy: Growing up in America's Ancient City*. Anaphora Literary Press. 2016.

Cutler, Robin R. *A Soul on Trial: A Marine Corps Mystery at the Turn of the Twentieth Century*. Lanham, MD: Rowman & Littlefield Publishers, Inc., 2007.

"Death Notices: 'Musterman on April 5, 1980, Lillian P.'" *Evening Capital*. April 7, 1980.

Doyel, Ginger. *Annapolis Vignettes*. Centerville, MD: Tidewater Press, 2005.

_____. "Life in the 1930s on College Avenue." *The Capital*. October 15, 2003.

Driscoll, Michael R. "Writer Reaches Back To His Mail Order Days." *The Baltimore Sun*. January 3, 1991. (https://www.baltimoresun.com/news/bs-xpm-1991-01-03-9113000054-story.html).

"Family discovers special edition of *Evening Capital* from more than 100 years ago," *The Capital*. April 1, 2016.

Felter, Mary. Personal communication: taped interview with Mrs. L.P. Musterman. Annapolis Convalescent Center. February 10, 1978.

"Fourteen Gather for Musterman Reunion." *Evening Capital*. July 17, 1953.

"Guest of Mrs. Musterman." *Evening Capital*. June 28, 1944.

"Hurricane Hazel Rips Through Annapolis." *Evening Capital*. October 16, 1954.

"In Annapolis: Reconciled by a Pardon." *Bay Weekly*. vol 9 No 26.

Works Cited

June 28–July 4, 2001. (https://bayweekly.com/old-site/year01/issue9_26/dock9_26.html).

Jaques, Frances. "Home of the Week, 'Victorian Style: House sparkling example of period.'" *The Capital.* October 10, 1987.

Klemesrud, Judy. "'Tea Fights' at Annapolis Introduces Plebes to Social Life." *New York Times.* May 6, 1969. (https://www.nytimes.com/1969/05/06/archives/-tea-fight-at-annapolis-introduces-plebes-to-social-life.html).

"Knighton, Cecil Claggett." *The Baltimore Sun.* July 14, 2007. (https://www.baltimoresun.com/news/bs-xpm-2006-07-14-0607140380-story.html).

"Local Zonta Club celebrates 50th year." *Evening Capital.* June 19, 1979.

"L.P. Musterman Hat Shop." photograph no. 84, *Annapolis Faces,* Annapolis Festival Foundation, Inc., not copyrighted, undated.

"L.P. Musterman Shop Is First One Finished." *Evening Capital.* October 18, 1961.

"Maryland Inventory of Historic Properties, Property AA-32 Baron de Kalb Monument." (https://mht.maryland.gov/secure/medusa/PDF/AnneArundel/AA-32.pdf).

"Maryland Inventory of Historic Properties, Property AA-574 195 Main Street." Maryland Historic Trust. (https://mht.maryland.gov/secure/medusa/PDF/AnneArundel/AA-574.pdf).

"Maryland Inventory of Historic Properties, Property AA-576 197 Main Street." Maryland Historic Trust. (https://mht.maryland.gov/secure/medusa/PDF/AnneArundel/AA-576.pdf).

"Maryland Inventory of Historic Properties, Property AA-581 [211 Main Street]." Maryland Historic Trust. (https://mht.maryland.gov/secure/medusa/PDF/AnneArundel/AA-581.pdf).

"Maryland Inventory of Historic Properties, Property AA-658 Feldmeyer-Gassaway House" [194 Prince George Street]. Maryland Historic Trust. (https://mht.maryland.gov/mihp/MIHPCard.aspx?MIHPNo=AA-658).

"Maryland Inventory of Historic Properties, Property AA-1324, 203-205 Main Street." Maryland Historic Trust. (https://mht.maryland.gov/secure/medusa/PDF/AnneArundel/AA-1324.pdf).

Matchett's Baltimore Directory for 1853–1854, Vol. 0564.

McIntire, Robert Harry. *Annapolis, Maryland, Families*. Baltimore, MD: Gateway Press. 1979.

McWilliams, Jane Wilson. *Annapolis, City on the Severn: A History*. Baltimore, MD: The Johns Hopkins University Press. Crownsville, MD: The Maryland Historical Trust Press, June 2011.

Miller, Ruby Young. "Recollections—Part II." *Anne Arundel County History Notes*. Vol. XXVIII, No. 4. July 1997.

"Millinery Opening." *Evening Capital*, September 28, 1918.

"More Flu Cases: Victims Increase." *Evening Capital*. October 2, 1918.

"Mrs. Musterman, Mother's Day Queen." Photo caption. *Evening Capital*. May 18, 1977.

Musterman, Lillian P. Personal communication. Letter to Kathryn Hayman Jackson. April 22, 1969.

"Newest Fashions In Winter Hats: Autumn Millinery Opening at the Holidayoke Company Today." *Evening Capital*, September 25, 1918.

"Notice of Hearing." *The Capital*. October 25, 2010.

"Notice of Meeting, 'Public Hearing and Deliberation, 1.'" *The Capital*. September 8, 2010.

Oakes, Amy. "Council Approves Mayor's Budget, 2001." *The Baltimore Sun*. May 23, 2000. (https://www.baltimoresun.com/news/bs-xpm-2000-05-23-0005230253-story.html).

Owings, Eleanor. "Musty, This Is Your Life." Script for Zonta's Ninetieth Birthday Celebration for Mrs. L.P. Musterman, December 1971, unpublished.

Passenger Information 1820–1872. National Archives. M255, Microfile roll 2, List No. 55.

Pidkowicz, Anne, personal communication, April 24, 2020.

Post, Emily. *Etiquette: the Blue Book of Social Usage*. Ninth Edition. New York: Funk & Wagnalls Co., 1958.

Reed, Elizabeth Leah. "From Appomattox to Alturas: The Journey of Nehemiah FitzGerald (1841–1905), First County Clerk of Modoc County As Revealed through His Letters." *Modoc County Historical Society*. No. 40. 2018.

_____. *We Come From Island People*. Petersrow, 2006. (https://petersrow.com/catalog/catalog.htm#A).

Reed, Nancy Musterman. Personal papers. Unpublished.

"Renewal Ideas Sought for West Street Buildings." *The Capital*. December 27, 2000.

Sanborn Fire Insurance Map, Annapolis, Anne Arundel County, Maryland. Sanborn Map Company. October, 1908. (https://www.loc.gov/item/sanborn03572_005/).

Serratore, Angela. "Keeping Feathers Off Hats—And On Birds," Smithsonianmag.com, May 15, 2018. (https://www.smithsonianmag.com/history/migratory-bird-act-anniversary-keeping-feathers-off-hats-180969077/).

Staff and Volunteers of Historic Annapolis, Inc. "Fact Sheets for Interpreters on Preservation, Restoration and History of Annapolis." 1967. unpublished.

Stevens, William Oliver. *Annapolis: Anne Arundel's Town*. New York: Dodd, Mead & Company, 1937.

"Stylish Display of Fall Millinery." *Evening Capital*. October 1, 1918.

Theobald, Sigrid. "Letters to the Editor, 'Mrs. Musterman's Gift.'" *Evening Capital*. June 29, 1967.

"Wanted 'Young lady … .' " *Evening Capital*. September 9, 1918.

Warren, Mame. *Then Again . . . Annapolis, 1900–1965*. Annapolis, MD: Time Exposures Limited, 1990.

Warren, Mame, and Marion Warren. *Everybody Works But John Paul Jones: A Portrait of the U.S. Naval Academy, 1845–1915*. Annapolis, MD: Naval Institute Press, 1981.

_____. *Maryland Time Exposures:1840–1940*. Baltimore, MD: The Johns Hopkins University Press, 1984.

Warren, Marion E., and Mame Warren. *The Train's Done Gone: An Annapolis Portrait, 1889–1910*. Annapolis, MD: Marion E. Warren, 1976.

Wollmershäuser, Friedrich R. "Passenger Departure Lists of German Emigrants, 1709–1914." Lecture handout papers. Spring 1997. (viewed but no longer available at: http://www.progenealogists.com/germany/articles/gdepart.htm).

White, Clarence Marbury, Sr., and Evangeline Kaiser White, *The Years Between: A Chronicle of Annapolis, Maryland, 1800-1900 and Memoirs of.* New York: Exposition Press, Inc., 1957.

"Zonta Member Honored." *Evening Capital.* December 16, 1971.

ACKNOWLEDGMENTS

*M*Y THANKS AND APPRECIATION go out to the many persons who made it possible for me to write the book I wanted to read. I am forever grateful to those who put pen to paper and voice to tape. My mother, Nancy Musterman Reed, left detailed memories of her childhood which filled in an otherwise unknown time period for me. Eleanor Owings talked with family members to gather, prepare, and present "Musty, This Is Your Life," at Lillian Musterman's 90th birthday celebration, which I attended. I found a copy of the presentation in my grandmother's papers. Kitty Burdett's story "The Magnificent Milliner" appeared in *The Annapolitan* and somehow found its way to my files. Mary Felter saw my name in *The Capital* in the 1990s and sent me the tape of her interview with my grandmother a year before her death. I gleaned details from all of these sources, as well as from innumerable searches of the *Evening Capital*'s online archives.

My mother's second cousin, Dorothy Beatty (née Hall)—a John Henry Musterman descendant through the Westphal family—helped me sort out the genealogy. She gave me an annotated copy of Andrew Jesse Musterman's family tree and pointed me to the late Raymond Disney. At Ray's dining room table in Annapolis, we huddled over the genealogy he compiled when he was stationed in Germany.

Thanks also to online members of Facebook's Friends of Annapolis group who never failed to make an interesting comment or respond to a follow up question whenever I posted a picture of the Milliner of Main Street. And my friends and colleagues who comprise The Rillito River Nonfiction Writers Group in Tucson, Arizona: thank you for your patience and insightful comments as you supported me and moved this book forward over the past too many years.

Special thanks to my cousin Peggy Houghton, for her generous support of this project. My great appreciation also extends to my cousin Sallie Nordskog, my sister Nancy Gesswein, and my daughter Dana Lillian Uehling, who added stories and reviewed various stages of the writing. And appreciation to my long-time colleagues and friends: Sheryl Sieracki for encouragement and advice over the years, and Suzanne Peake for the final edit.

And finally, thank you dear husband Bill Casey. You stood by me with your usual good humor during many wanderings through graveyards and buildings, waited patiently as I shot just one more picture, listened to oft-repeated stories, and read draft after draft during the past seven years.

Thank you all.

ABOUT THE AUTHOR

*E*LIZABETH LEAH REED IS a nonfiction writer whose work has appeared in *Leaping Clear, J. of the Modoc County Historical Society, Oasis J., Taijiquan J., Inside Annapolis*, and others. Her earlier book, *We Come from Island People* (Petersrow, 2000), chronicles the history and genealogies of five families of the Eastern Shore of Virginia from 1645 to 1900. She graduated from the University of Maryland, was an award-winning corporate writer, taught at George Washington University, and cofounded what is now the Annapolis Maritime Museum. She visits Annapolis, Maryland, her former hometown, 'most every year, leaving for a while the heat of her desert residence in Tucson, Arizona, where she writes, birds, and practices tai chi.

∿

Any additional information, stories, and corrections pertaining to Mrs. Musterman or the information in this biography and the appendixes will be greatly appreciated. Please forward to eleahreed@gmail.com.

A Note on the Type

This book was set in a version of Monotype Baskerville, the antecedent of which was a typeface designed by John Baskerville (1706–1775). Baskerville, a writing master in Birmingham, England, began experimenting around 1750 with type design and punch cutting and became known as a master type-founder and printer. Baskerville's types, which are distinctive and elegant in design, are considered transitional typefaces that bridge classical typefaces and the high contrast modern faces, thus they were forerunners of what we know today as modern typefaces.

Made in the USA
Middletown, DE
14 July 2021

44142257R00123